The Gift

Larry E. Taylor

Introduction

Knowing this first, that there shall come in the last days scoffers, walking after their own lusts. II Peter 3:3

Speaking of Israel: Thus saith the Lord God to the prophet Ezekiel nearly 600 years before the birth of Christ:

And I will bring them out from the people, and gather them from the countries, and will bring them to their own land, and feed them upon the mountains of Israel by the rivers, and all the inhabited places of the country. Ezekiel 34:13

Since May 14, 1948 the world has been witnessing the process of that prophecy being fulfilled before our very eyes and scoffing has increased to the point that it is indeed extremely rare to hear anyone mention God with any respect at all.

This book is in essence an autobiography but it is more than that. It is the testimony of how God brought about the granting of a very specific request by the author. During the time that it took to do so I experienced several "kairos" moments.

I was also preserved through various circumstances described in the back of the book for what

I believe to probably be the major purpose of my life—To write this book.

Larry E Taylor

Contents

Let the redeemed of the Lord say so.

Psalms 101: 2

Conclusion

Background

For God so loved the world, that he gave his only begotten son, that whosoever believeth in him should not perish, but have everlasting life.

John 3:16

I grew up in the small village of Plymouth, Ohio, located midway between Cleveland and Columbus on the Huron/Richland county line.

It was the home of the Fate, Root, Heath Company, the largest employer in the village. The shop whistle could be heard all over the village at 7:00 am, noon, 12:30pm, and 3:30pm. It was the manufacturing site of the Plymouth locomotive, Silver King tractors, lawn mowers, and clay machinery used for making various porcelain products.

It was a very vibrant community during the time that I lived there. There was a mixture of the old and the new: hitching posts lined the sidewalks, there was a saddle shop, a blacksmith that shod horses, and many retail stores for such a small community.

I would estimate the population was between 1200 and 1500 people during the 1940s.

The village had two medical doctors, a dentist, three barbers, a volunteer fire department, and at least two policemen.

Retail stores included a dress shop, five and dime store, at least two meat/grocery stores, a dry goods store, one or two jewelry stores, a confectionary, a student hangout called the Hitching Post, two hardware stores, and two electronic stores.

There were also two saloons, one with a pool hall, and the village also had an indoor/outdoor movie theater, whose owner had outdoor movies on Wednesday nights, using the side of the building as the screen.

Within the village there were four churches representing the major denominations: a Catholic Church along with Lutheran, Methodist, and a Presbyterian. All were very well attended.

The public school, which had been built in 1929, serviced grades 1 through 12 in 1946 when I entered first grade. There was also a private kindergarten which I attended.

There were at least two gasoline stations in the village, one of which my grandfather owned or managed. My father worked several years for him while attending high school and for a few years after he graduated.

The village also had a lumber yard, a granary, and a cement block manufacturing company.

There are two diagonal roads entering the village business district from the east side. In the center of the north/south highway passing through the business area there was a traffic light mounted on a concrete base. The base was probably two or three feet square on the bottom and was positioned on the Huron/Richland county line. The base had walls that beveled upward nearly six feet high forming a top probably eighteen to twenty-four inches square for the light to set on. This light was commonly referred to as the dummy.

From the dummy the road continued west as one road. It crossed over the Baltimore and Ohio railroad track via a bridge at the western end of the business district.

A narrow concrete alley 30 to 40 feet long led from the southwest part of the village square sidewalk back to a small landing area to the front door of our two story apartment. On the west side of the alley was the dress shop. As the alley came to our front door landing it ended, but there was a small path that continued south to the small backyard behind our apartment.

On the front east corner of the alley there were 2 or 3 steps up to a door which opened to the stairway leading up to the apartment above the barber shop below. The two apartments were connected by a door on the second floor of our apartment.

As I remember, the front door of our apartment entered the living room area and there were wide stairs on the left which led to the upstairs. The living room area had a pot bellied coal stove separating it from the kitchen area in the back. The stairs led up to the bathroom and two connecting bedrooms. From the kitchen on the first floor there was a door that opened to the backyard.

The apartment next to ours had a beautiful front porch from which you could see most of the business area of the town. Across the street was the telephone company building. The first floor contained numerous switchboards with chairs in front of them. Many women were employed as operators servicing the primarily party lines that existed at that time.

The telephone building is still standing and has a wide metal stairway leading up to an apartment above the first floor. Friends of my mother lived there when I was young.

I was born in May 1940 and the earliest event of my life that I remember was getting my first haircut. I had to have been less than two years old as my mother was expecting my brother Bill, who was born 2 years and 2 months after me.

We entered the shop and sat down waiting my turn. I watched the barber sharpening his straight razor and applying steamy hot towels to the face of the man in the barber chair. I watched the barber stir the soap in a mug with a small brush and apply it to the man's face. He then began to shave the man very carefully with the straight razor. When he was finished, he took one of the numerous bottles of lotion from a shelf near him and applied a small amount to his face.

The next gentleman got in the chair and he only wanted a haircut. The electric scissors made a lot of noise and rather frightened me. He soon was done and it was my turn.

The barber reached to the side of the barber chair and picked up a black booster seat that was made to stay in place on the seat of the barber chair. It was a board that extended across both arms of the barber chair and had a base that sat directly on the seat of the barber chair that prevented it from sliding around. It was fully upholstered with a black leather covering.

My mother picked me up and sat me on the seat. When the barber turned on the electric clippers, I went ballistic. He called to my mother to try to hold me while he proceeded to cut my hair as best he could. I screamed throughout the process and with a sigh of relief he handed me to my mother. It took at least another time or two before I was no longer frightened by the clippers.

My brother was born in July 1942 and I remember several things that took place when I was 3 or 4 years old. One morning I went through the upstairs door over to my friend Ray's apartment. His mother prepared eggs for breakfast and I think that it was the first time I had eggs for breakfast. Ray's father did not drink coffee. He had a large glass of milk. In addition to the eggs, I also acquired a major taste for bananas.

The village merchants went all out for the youngsters during the Christmas season. All were invited to the theater for the arrival of Santa Claus. I remember entering the theater to a packed attendance of an anxiously waiting group of kids. Santa Claus arrived and handed a bag of candy to each of us.

By the time Bill reached a year old he was walking very well. On occasion, he would pick up a pencil or crayon and write on the wall. Mother decided to purchase each of us blackboards for Christmas one year in hopes of getting Bill to stop writing on the wall.

Bill and I shared a bedroom upstairs. I had a small bed and he had a crib next to the wall. Shortly after Christmas mother put us down for our afternoon naps. As I was looking around the room I saw that Bill had messed his diaper and was standing in his crib and reaching in his diaper and spreading feces all over the wall!

I called to mother and when she entered the bedroom and saw what was taking place, she walked directly to the newly purchased blackboards that were on tripods and picked them up and slammed them to the floor shattering the slate into hundreds of pieces. I thought "Happy New Year—Thanks Bill." I learned very young that life is not always fair. I believe that was a portent of a far more serious event which would occur several years later.

Wednesday nights were shopping nights. A mixture of horse and buggies and automobiles filled the shopping area with the horses tied to the hitching rails. As dusk arrived people would migrate to the field beside the movie theater where the owner provided outdoor movies.

The U.S. had entered World War II after the attack on Pearl Harbor and I do not remember any of the movies or previews that I saw, but I will never forget the newsreels that were shown before the movies. The pictures of war terrified me. As the war progressed, all the lights had to be turned off at dusk for fear of bombing raids.

Hitler was hung in effigy and set on fire further terrifying me. Rationing was in effect for many food-stuffs and gasoline. We saved tin foil and wrapped it into balls for the war effort. Everyone gave a big sigh of relief and gave thanks when the war ended in August 1945.

Life returned to somewhat normal after the war and I entered kindergarten. We made drums out of oatmeal cartons, began learning the alphabet, and sang songs. It became very apparent that I had no music ability as I could not keep tune with my class-mates. I began to keep quiet and as much as I enjoy music I remain silent when others sing.

I learned many things during my year in kinder-garten but one thing I learned outside of kinder-garten was this: stay out of the way when men or women are working. A friend of my father had come to the apartment to help him replace a stovepipe on the stove. I was standing nearby, when they dropped it, and it hit my right hand leaving a scar on the side of my hand which lasted for well over 50 years, reminding me of the occasion.

Kindergarten ended, the summer was over, and it was time to enter first grade. First grade was at the high school and as we entered the building we were shown to our classroom. We were seated at bench like tables and the teacher introduced herself and began speaking. I have no idea what she said but after listening to her for a half hour or less I thought to myself: "This is not for me. How am I ever going to make it through 12 years of school?" Things and my attitude improved and I made it through that year and it was time for summer fun.

That first year of school I became friends of many other students that I had not known. On occasion, we would get together and play tag in the evening. The yard in back of our apartment adjoined the yard of one of the doctor's in town and his wife always had beautiful tulips in the spring. It also had a rather long clothesline directly in back of our yard.

One evening as we were playing tag I was running very hard and forgot about the clothesline. I ran directly into it hitting the line in the center of my throat and my feet went up in the air and I landed with a thud. The line had not broken but I was very sore for a few days.

Another thing that I remember from that summer was playing superman with my friend Jim. He lived in a rather large home with a small barn which had a garage and a second floor with an opening on the side overlooking the yard below. We would put on capes and may have held umbrellas as we jumped nearly ten feet to the ground below. I think that we did that only once as it was quite a jump and we landed hard, but did not injure ourselves.

Saturday evenings were also shopping nights. Residents and others filled the square on those nights and, after shopping, were blessed with a band concert by a band from a neighboring community. Sometimes other bands would participate and the entertainment was well appreciated.

I believe it was the summer between my first and second grades that our mother took my brother

Bill to see her friend that lived above the telephone company. While they were there her friend gave Bill a copy of the New Testament. I was a little hurt that I did not get one but later that year or the next I received one from the Gideons. I recall reading John 3:16 and signing my name attesting to my belief in God. A few years ago I gave that testament to an organization that was collecting Bibles to be smuggled into countries where Christians are not allowed.

Our mother was a first cousin to former Baseball Commissioner Ford Frick. Sometime during my second year of school our parents took Bill to Indiana to visit relatives. When they returned all Bill could talk about was having bread and milk with Uncle Jake, Ford's father who was in his ninety's. Bill wanted to be like Uncle Jake and have bread and milk every night before going to bed so that he too could live to be that age.

Summer once more arrived and I had successfully completed two years of school—10 more to go!

My friend Jim's father had given him a two wheeled bicycle for his eighth birthday. His father spent an afternoon patiently teaching each of us how to ride it. He was one of the most patient men I have ever known.

That same summer Jim's mother took us to the swimming pool in the park at Shelby. We had to get up early but were soon very wide awake as we entered that cold water for Red Cross swimming lessons. The first lesson began with teaching us how to float on our backs. Jim progressed very well and was soon a very competent swimmer by the end of the six weeks of lessons held once per week. I, on the other hand, could not float on my back and learned nothing. One day that same summer the Lutheran pastor's son ran away. When Rick's father could not find him he enlisted the help of various people. We had been looking for Rick calling his name very loudly for quite some time and everyone became very concerned. I could not believe that Rick had run very far away. He was several years younger than me and I began searching the bushes next to the church. It was not long until I found him and I said: "Rick, why?" He never answered but all were very relieved that he had been found.

Sundays were very quiet in those days. The "Blue Laws" were still observed and all businesses were closed. Gas stations were probably open but few, if any, restaurants. Our village had two elderly policemen that were not very visible on Sundays. Even during the week truckers tended to speed through the town.

There were many Sunday afternoons when several young men riding on motorcycles would come into town carrying several cartons of beer in glass bottles. They would park their motorcycles and would carry their beer up the metal stairs by the telephone company and sit down. They would sit there for a half hour or more drinking their beer and throwing the empty bottles all over the sidewalk. When the beer was gone they would jump on their cycles and leave.

I watched that same scenario on many Sundays for two or three years until a tough young man, probably newly discharged from service, arrived from Cleveland to become the new police chief. He had been a golden glove boxing champ and was a very good marksman with the two pistols that hung very low in the holsters hanging from his belt.

I was sitting on a bench by myself on what was probably his first Sunday as chief. He drove the police cruiser into town several minutes after the motorcyclists had drunk their first beer and had thrown the bottles on the sidewalk. He got out of the car and walked up to them and told them to get out of town. They gathered their beer and got on their cycles to leave. When they reached the dummy they stopped their cycles and decided to challenge the new young chief.

Bob pulled those two pistols from their holsters with lightening speed and fired two shots one of which I am quite sure hit one of the cyclists. While doing so he told them again to get out of town and not come back. They were gone in an instant and the town was cleaned up in a day. Word spread fast and there was no more speeding through the village.

The longer he served the greater his reputation grew as being a very good police officer that was absolutely fearless. He was called to help get an escaped prisoner out of a barn one night. When he arrived he entered the barn by himself and soon came out with the prisoner.

My parents became very good friends with Bob and his wife and I was very thankful for what he had done to make our village safe. I had very high respect for him and he always spoke to me when he saw me.

September 1948 arrived and I entered the third grade. Bill began first grade. Mother had told us to expect a new brother or sister in the near future and we were excited about that. Our sister Anita arrived in November and an event took place soon after that would change our lives forever.

The Event

Trust in the Lord with all thine heart: and lean not unto thine own understanding.
Proverbs 3:5

She stood at the white porcelain sink, full of despair, glancing into the mirror and down to the sink, slowly turning to red as the blood flowed from her wrists which she had sliced. *

My brother and I learned of this event when our grandmother and her daughter came to pick us up at school. They took us to their house where we waited for our father to arrive from work.

We sat and starred on and off at the flames of the gas stove saying very little as the wind howled outside while the snow continued to fall heavily as we waited that day shortly before Thanksgiving 1948.

Our sister was about two weeks old and grandmother held her in her arms rocking in the rocking chair singing: "What a Friend We Have in Jesus" and other songs of comfort as we waited.

- May not be accurate narrative. Fourteen years ago, a few months before our father

21

died, and I already had many notes for this book, I asked him if he could give me some details about this event. I did not tell him that I was planning to write a book. At 86 years old and over 50 years later, it was too painful to discuss. I know how he felt.

Our father arrived at the house after dark and after being told what happened he sat in stunned silence. He at last spoke and uttered some of the most disconsolate words I have ever heard: "Well, I guess I'll have to take the kids to the children's home."

After what seemed to be an eternity, my grandmother spoke and said in a very quiet voice: "we are not going to do that." The details are fuzzy but mother ended up in the state mental institution for six months. Our family never spent another night together under the same roof.

If I remember correctly our father was working in Cleveland at that time and was gone during the week. My grandfather was working construction work and he too was gone a lot. Many times when Bill and I returned from school our grandmother would be in the rocking chair holding our sister and singing: "The Old Rugged Cross." She called on our Savior often to get us through that time.

Our father's oldest sister was married in 1948 or 1949 and our sister went to be with her and her husband for a period of time. When our mother was released from the hospital my father and brother went to be with her and her father. I remained at my grandmother's house until I graduated from high school. I did eat most of my meals with my parents and the rest of the family.

It was two months before we were allowed our first visit to see mother. I went with dad on the long trip to Columbus via the two lane highway before the interstate highway was built.

As we went into the hospital, we did not know what to expect. Mother, I'm sure had not expected to be alive, and would be concerned about what our reaction would be.

It was a very awkward meeting. It was as if we were total strangers. I'm not sure that she was happy to see us. I don't remember any hugs given. She had lost weight and still had a long way to go before she would be normal.

She told us about receiving electrical shock treatment, which was very barbaric in those days, and is still used today for some patients. Thankfully, there are many new medications available today that have various degrees of success. It was a short visit and I felt very bad for my father as we returned home.

Living with a mentally ill patient is an experience of its own. You never know what will happen or when it will occur. You ask yourself:

"Did I do something to cause this?" "Is it a chemical imbalance that caused it?" You are always trying to come up with an answer.

When our mother returned home to her father's home my sister, brother, and father joined them. My sister at a very young age often was the mother to our mother. I only ate meals there and was not aware of many things that took place.

Mother was in and out of the hospital several more times following that first hospitalization, but she did have probably ten or twelve years of "normal" life between 32 and 74 years of age before passing on in 1991.

Over the years, I rarely discussed this part of my life. My wife is a nurse, and was very involved with the doctor who treated my mother after my parents moved to Mansfield. That treatment contributed heavily to the: "Good years" that mother enjoyed.

Several years ago we were involved in a discussion with a nurse friend, and she suggested that I might like to read two books written by M. Scott Peck. Dr. Peck had many years of experience treating patients with mental illness and I tend to agree with his assessment. The names of his books are "The Road Less Traveled and People of the Lie." I would highly recommend them if you are interested in the subject.

There is a certain "stigma" associated with mental illness that does not exist with physical illness. As the child of a mentally ill mother I always felt very inadequate. I could not wait to disassociate myself from my environment. There was never anything said to me, but it was an innate feeling that existed for many years. Before my brother died, he told our daughter that he had experienced that same feeling.

This "stigma" was confirmed over 50 years later in a discussion with our friends Jim and Dixie. Our high school had made plans for a 50 year reunion of the football team which had an undefeated season one year. I was looking forward to seeing many players that I had not seen in years. One of them was our right halfback, Jim, who I had seen only once since he graduated.

Several days after receiving my invitation, I had a call from our quarterback, Ray, telling me about Jim. He had been in a hospital and had been released for a short visit home. After speaking to a friend of his, he walked to a 10 story building and jumped off. When I told Jim and Dixie about this, her reply was: "What do you expect? His father had killed himself." His brother told me that his invitation had arrived later that same day!

From The Golfer's Guide to Life April 1, 2011: The best thing we can do about our tough breaks is to play them with determined acceptance, and play them where they lie.

Jack Nicholas

Decision

Fear not: for I am with thee; be not dismayed; for I am thy God: I will strengthen thee; yea I will help thee, yea I will uphold thee with the right hand of my righteousness.

Isaiah 41:10

It was a beautiful Sunday afternoon the middle of March 1949. I had gone to Columbus with my father on Saturday to pick up my mother for her first home visit since entering the hospital. I had gone to her father's home where dad and she were staying. I am not sure if Bill was there but Anita was not.

We had eaten lunch and we were sitting in the living room and dad and she were talking prior to him taking her back to Columbus. I don't know what they were discussing but all of a sudden she picked up a pair of shoes and threw them violently at him.

I walked out of the house and began walking up to the village business area. As I was walking across the railroad trestle there was a train approaching and the steam engine's whistle was blowing. I stopped on that bridge and looked at that train coming down the track and thought to myself: "Should I just end it all now and jump in front of that train?" And I thought "No, with God's help, I am going to live my life to the absolute fullest no matter what my environment."

I became somewhat hard after that decision but I have lived by it ever since I made it two months before turning 9 years old!

Girl on a Horse

*I will instruct thee and teach thee in the way
thou shalt go; I will guide thee with mine eye.*
Psalms 32:8

School began again after that very painful Thanksgiving week. I somehow made it through third grade. One of the first things that my father did after mother went into the hospital was to take me to the clothing store and introduce me to the salesman. He told me that when I need clothes to see him and get what I wanted. I have been purchasing clothes on my own since I have been 8 years old.

My aunt had a girl after she was married and she had her hands full with her and my sister. My grandmother did not want me to stay by myself at 9 years old and she would take me along when she went to help her daughter. I would just get to sleep and she would wake me up to go home. I finally asked her to leave me at home alone.

My grandmother had a beautiful Springer Spaniel named Spot. Spot and I bonded instantly and we had no problem staying in the house by ourselves. I was 10 or 11 years old when Spot died of poisoning. We never found out how that happened, but it broke my heart.

While staying at grandmother's house, I developed a very good friendship with one of my classmates who lived in the house behind my grandmother's. Mick had 5 brothers and later a sister.

I don't know how it began but Mick and I made it a habit to attend the Presbyterian Church on Sundays. We would go to Sunday school and we stayed for the church service. The teachers had a sincere interest in young people and hosted various activities for us. Going to the skating rink in Mansfield was one my favorite things to do.

One summer Mick and I attended summer camp at The College of Wooster and stayed in the dormitory. It was very well attended and we had a good time meeting new people, hearing very good lectures, and participating in many activities.

We continued to attend church services through high school. I don't remember one message from the pulpit but I will always remember how the minister began his lecture. He never failed to recite Psalms 19:14 "Let the words of my mouth and the meditation of my heart, be acceptable in thy sight, O Lord, my strength, and my redeemer."

During that time we were given eight Sunday school books that I never read. I kept them for over 50 years, determined to read them before I died. Mission accomplished in 2014. They were very good books and I passed them on to a friend who had also attended the church.

My tendency to procrastinate, at times, probably developed from burying myself in many activities to avoid any thoughts of the "stigma". There were many times during my school years when I would be sitting at my desk wearing only Jockey shorts, cramming for a test. That upstairs bedroom was so cold in the winter that the water in a shoeshine polish lid on my desk would freeze solid. My concentration would be so intense that I never got cold.

My grandmother had a party for my 10th birthday. It was a small party attended by three or four boys. I received my first ball glove and a Plumb hatchet from my grandfather. I still use that hatchet on occasion.

Jim's father was taking him to Mansfield for an evening meal to celebrate his 10th birthday and I was invited to join them. I had Salisbury steak for the first time in my life. I had eaten it rather quickly and Jim's father asked if I would like to have some more. I was reluctant to say yes and he ordered more for me. Jim's family was very generous to me and I enjoyed many marvelous times with them.

I went on my first train ride by myself that summer. I rode the train from Willard to either Rome or Peru, Indiana to spend a week with my aunt and uncle at their trailer home located on a nearby lake. The ride was several hours long and the conductor checked on me quite frequently.

I had a very good time with my aunt and uncle and especially enjoyed fishing for sucker fish that my uncle would use for bait to catch northern pike. All of us also had fun fishing for crappie.

We went to their home in Tipton and also to their daughter's home in Kokomo. We did many other things and the week passed quickly. I was taken to the train to return home for the rest of the summer.

Sometime that summer Jim and I began working for the owner of one of the hardware stores. He owned a farm and also raised sheep. The first day of work we were riding on a flat bed wagon that was being pulled by a small Ford tractor driven by Beryl, the owner of the farm. He would stop frequently, and we would jump off the wagon to pick up rocks that were in the field, and throw them on the wagon.

After working in a given area we would get on the wagon and move to a new location. I was sitting on the side of the wagon, letting my foot drag against the wheel, when we hit a bump and my foot got under the wheel and I was drug off the wagon. The ground was soft and I was not hurt. I quickly jumped back on the wagon before I was seen.

In addition to that work, I would work several hours a week mowing their rather large lawn. During the fall I would put toys together for the Christmas Season.

Jim and I had some good times working together over three or four years. One summer, we painted a very long fence. Another summer, we helped Beryl build a road through the woods. We also helped him build a beach for the small lake that was on the farm.

One summer, Jim and I pitched a fairly large tent on a plateau and slept on cots for most of the summer. At night we would ride our bikes to the drive in movie.

One night after returning from the movie, we went for a swim in the pond. It was a very clear night and all of a sudden the sky lit up very bright. Workers were pouring steel at the steel mill in Mansfield over 20 miles away but it still lit up the whole sky.

I will forever be grateful for what Mr. M taught me during those few years when I was young. In addition to working for Beryl, I mowed lawn for10 or 12 other people during the summer and shoveled snow for many of them in the winter.

I also enjoyed doing many other things. I had finished seventh grade before learning to swim. I rode my bike to a pond several miles outside of the village to meet four or five other boys. There was a high school student there named Mac, who took me aside and taught me to swim in less than 5 minutes! When I told him about not being able to float on my back, he told me to take a deep breath, put my face down in the water, and start moving my arms. I soon was diving into deep water with the rest of them.

One winter, Jim and I along with several other boys were walking on a river that was frozen over, and I suddenly broke through the ice. The river was fairly deep and one of them caught me before I went under the water. Another time, Jim and I went to a pond on a very warm spring day and decided to go for a swim even though there was still ice around the edge. When I went in and went under the water I came up and called to Jim not to come in because the cold nearly paralyzed me. He went in anyway.

Another time we were swimming in a pond where there were cattle in the field. We were in the water when several girls took our clothes and were running away when the cattle decided to come into the pond. We ran out of the water and climbed a tree with our bare butts hanging just above the cattle with their horns just below us as they entered the water.

When we were in junior high school, Jim and I joined the Boy Scouts and began working on merit badges. We were heavy into it and were able to go to summer camp. Jim received his life saving merit badge during our first year at camp. After learning to swim, I began my life saving lessons the following year.

The instructor was very good. During the week he kept emphasizing to us that we must follow his instructions. A person about to drown would most likely cause us to drown if we did not approach him properly. The first scout jumped into the water to attempt to save our instructor. He did everything wrong and the instructor soon had him in a headlock holding him under the water. After nearly drowning him, he helped him to the deck. Needless to say he failed the test.

After watching five or six other scouts not following instructions and getting nearly drowned, I jumped into the water, determined that it would not happen to me. I soon had the instructor locked in a cross body hold that he could not get out of, even though he was biting my forearm. At the end of the morning and passing very few scouts, the instructor asked me if I would like to serve as a life guard the following year. I explained that I would not be able to do so because of my work commitments. It was a very good confidence building experience for me.

Neither Jim nor I attained the Eagle rank, but we did earn nearly 20 merit badges each, and both of us attained the rank of Life. I also became a den chief helping with Cub scouts and Jim later became a scoutmaster.

In addition to all of my other activities, I began playing basketball during upper elementary school. When I entered junior high school, I began getting involved with many pick-up games. We had a very good junior high team and because of my leaping ability, I acquired a nickname that I did not like and will not reveal.

There was one student a year or two older than the rest of us in our class. He began picking on me for no reason and would hit me quite often. I determined that I would handle it without direct confrontation, when I got a little older. I arranged for a three on three football game one morning before school and invited him to play. Of course we were playing without equipment and when he was carrying the ball I hit him with all I had burying my shoulder in his ribs. He went down with a thud and that was the last physical confrontation I had in school.

I was walking across the street one day while in the eighth grade on my way to the barber shop where I enjoyed listening to the barber and the postman debate the merits of various automobiles while waiting for my turn. A gentleman, who was a very successful businessman, approached me and asked me a question: "Ed, do you think you will ever amount to anything?" That question has burned in my heart since he asked it, and I'm not sure if I answered him, because of such high respect I had for him.

It was about a month before high school football practice would begin my freshman year. I had gone to have lunch with my family, and we were sitting there talking, when I heard the sound of horses coming down the street.

I went outside to see two younger girls riding and they were handling the horses very well. I noticed the one girl in particular with her beautiful auburn hair that nearly matched the color of the horse she was riding. She was the younger daughter of the postman I enjoyed listening to at the barber shop. I made up my mind that when we were both older, I would ask her for a date.

High School

Let the words of my mouth and the meditation of my heart be acceptable in thy sight, o Lord my strength, and my redeemer.
Psalms 19:14

August 20, 1954 my high school football career began. I will never forget that first practice. Coach K was probably six feet tall and weighed 200 pounds and could punt the ball like a NFL kicker. He could whisper and be heard in a neighboring village.

As he walked over the hill, looking down to the field, where 21 or 22 young men dressed in full pads were standing, his first words were: "Start running." After running one or two miles around the football field with him yelling to run faster, he called us to line up at the bottom of the hill, which he had walked down.

He then told us to line up with the bleachers to charge up to a tree about 15 or 20 yards up the hill. After charging up that hill for eight or ten times, he ordered us to line up for calisthenics, which he led for a half hour or more. We did not touch a football, until we were near exhaustion, from all of that rigorous exercise.

When calisthenics were over, he divided the ends and backs from the rest of the team. He would then send a back or an end down the field to catch one of his 60 or 70 yard punts. As he was kicking the ball, two tacklers were to run down the field to tackle the runner. If the runner did not get through the tacklers, he had to run around the field. If the tacklers did not make the tackle, they began running. Soon everyone was running again. This drill lasted for at least a half hour.

We were then taught how to block and tackle properly, and practiced doing so for 15 to 20 minutes, before proceeding to learn some basic offensive plays. We would be playing a single wing offense that year and there was no playbook to study. We concentrated on learning and executing plays over and over until we had them mastered before our first game.

This very demanding practice program continued and when it was time for our first game, we were down to twelve or thirteen players, to play a seven game season. We were playing with eleven players on each team, which meant that most of us played the entire game. I had six blisters on one foot and seven on the other, and my father insisted that I not play that game. I left home to meet the bus for our trip to Brunswick. Brunswick was a larger school, but not nearly as large as it is today.

During the second quarter of the game our wingback suffered a broken neck and we went the season with twelve players! Even though most of us played both offence and defense for each game, we looked forward to it. Games were a piece of cake compared to our practices. We finished the season with two wins and five losses.

That physical training was the most rigorous of my life and I am most grateful, for it as it has given me the discipline to continue with some type of exercise program for over sixty years. I know our former quarterback does the same.

The following year, we had two young coaches, who switched our offense to a split T and our record improved to 5 wins and 2 losses. My junior year, we were undefeated and I don't know what our record was for my senior year, as I missed one or two games due to injury.

I continued with my determination to bury myself with activities and take as many classes as possible. When my mother saw my class schedule, unknown, until many years later, I was told by someone that she had called the school superintendent to voice her concern. He and his family lived across the street from my grandmother's house, where I slept at night, and he told my mother to let me do whatever I wanted to do and that I would get through it. It turned out that he gave her good advice, for I accomplished what I wanted to do.

In addition to taking academic courses during my school career I took two courses that have been of great benefit all my life. I had an excellent shop teacher who taught us the fundamentals of electricity, working with the various wood working tools, making patterns for various iron castings, and basic drawing. For my shop project, I made a walnut desk lamp with some assistance from the instructor, which I have on my desk.

Typing class was taught by a teacher who taught business communications in addition to teaching us keyboarding skills. I am thankful for all that I learned from such a fine teacher.

When it became obvious that I planned to participate in as many sports that I could, our father purchased the York 200 barbell set for Bill and I to train with. Bob Huffman was the Olympic weight trainer at that time and we used a book written by him to begin our training. Bill and I trained hard that summer and both of us became much stronger.

Bill and I never really fought with each other, probably because of being separated when I was eight years old and he was six. We did have a slight altercation as a result of what I did to him.

I had purchased a BB gun, and on some afternoons when no one was home I would lie in bed and shoot at a plastic chicken sitting on a shelf hanging on the wall.

Bill and I were sitting on the bed one afternoon, and for whatever reason, I doubled the blanket, and put it on his thigh and shot him, to see if it hurt. He stood up and was furious. When I stood up, he hit me with his balled up fist directly under my chin. I went air born for three or four feet hitting the wall and fell crashing to the floor. I was not hurt, but was so angry, that I dared not hit him because I deserved it.

I love music; particularly trumpet music, and I wanted to become another Harry James. At the beginning of my sophomore year I approached my mother about taking trumpet lessons. My uncle had an old trumpet from his high school years and let me use it. I contacted the music instructor and he agreed to give me lessons. As I am prone to do, once I become focused, I go all out. I would come home from football practice and would not eat until I had practiced playing the trumpet for at least an hour.

I continued trying to become a trumpet player and eventually played in the concert band during the winter months. After practicing so hard, I became unable to play the trumpet, and my music instructor suggested I try the saxophone. I did, but it soon became apparent that no matter how hard I tried, I did not have the talent to become a musician. Sometime during my junior year I gave up. The Good Lord knew what I would have done had I become a good trumpet player. I would probably have become a drunk playing on a river boat.

Not too long after I began taking trumpet lessons, the daughter of one of the doctors in town began calling me. She would call me when I was practicing and I would ask her not to call. After several attempts, she gave up.

However she did help me in a way that I am not proud of. I had such a course load that I only had two study halls for a week of school. I was taking sophomore literature, and we were required to read several books and make oral book reports. I am not sure how it started, but Vaughn D'Lee began to read the books, and write reports for me, which I would use for doing my oral reports. I don't think I read any of the required books, but I apparently did a good job with the oral reports because I had no problem with passing the class.

One morning before lunch, we were in biology class dissecting a cat that one of our classmates had brought to class. One of the girls, dressed to the hilt, was standing in the back of the room watching as one of the boys began stretching the intestine out of the cat's body. It broke and snapped back landing all over her. I had a difficult time enjoying lunch.

In the spring of that year I decided that it was time to ask the girl on a horse for a date. She was now in the eighth grade and there was a good movie playing in Mansfield. When I asked her, she told me that she would have to check with her parents. Her parents told her that they would prefer having me come to their home for dinner, and that they would take us to the movie.

When I arrived for dinner, I became aware that it was a home filled with love and respect for each other. It was a home that I wanted to have some day. I don't remember what the movie was about but I had a wonderful time that evening. Carol was a beautiful young girl and I loved her and her family very much and I know they liked me. However, such a feeling of total inadequacy engulfed me, because of the "stigma" that I determined that I would never become seriously involved with anyone from Plymouth.

I continued helping the hardware store owner and also began helping many farmers in the area bale hay. It was hard work but I enjoyed it. One farmer had eight or ten workers helping him and after a hard morning's work, he had us come into the house for lunch. That lunch had been prepared by his daughter, who was in the eighth grade. Marlene was a very accomplished cook and lunch was appreciated by all.

My friend, Ray, decided to discontinue working for the local milkman and asked me if I would like to have his job. I said yes, and he introduced me to George, the owner. I helped him every Saturday morning from 6:00am until afternoon.

After working several months, George asked me if I would babysit with their two young children. I hesitated with my reply, and he assured me that they would be in bed asleep when I arrived. When I entered their home, he took me to their refrigerator and showed me all the food that his wife had pre-pared and told me to eat whatever I wanted. He told me where he and his wife would be and gave me a phone number to reach them if I needed some-thing. He said that they would be home shortly after midnight. He paid me very well and gave me plenty to eat and drink, while I spent the evening watching television or reading a book. What a deal!

If memory serves me correctly, we were given aptitude tests our sophomore year and I scored very high in five different areas and very low in art and music. I enjoy both very much, but was not blessed with talent for either one.

I have been very thankful for our high school English teacher, Ms. Easterday, who went out of her way to introduce students to various plays held at the Huron playhouse.

I tried out for the play "Professor How Could You" my junior year and was awarded the lead part. What an experience that was. I spent hours learning the lines and when we performed the play the first time in front of a fairly large audience my friend Mick began reciting lines from act three in act one! Try to improvise that in front of a live audience. We made our way through it and I never heard anyone comment, so they were either very nice or didn't know the difference.

Jim and I had a couple of interesting experiences while in high school. One evening six or seven boys climbed into his father's Cadillac to go to Shelby. On the return trip, Jim was driving very fast and we went air born as we crested a hill. Another Jim, who was sitting in the front middle seat, reached for the ignition switch and turned the engine off. When Jim turned the engine back on, both mufflers blew making an unbelievable loud noise at 1:30am or 2:00am in the morning.

As we approached his home, we stopped several hundred yards away and pushed the car with the engine off to the front of the garage. Jim went quietly inside and opened the garage door for the rest of us to put the car inside. I can just imagine the thoughts his father must have had when he turned the engine on to go to work that morning!

Jim asked if I would like to go water skiing and I told him that I would like to but had never skied before. We met his parents at Lake Erie where they had a cottage with a channel going out to the lake. We boarded their fairly large cabin cruiser and headed for the lake. Jim began skiing and was a very proficient skier. After Jim had skied for quite a while, his father asked me if I would like to try and of course I did. I am guessing that his father's boat engine consumed at least a quarter tank of gasoline before I was able to finally get on top of the water.

I would go periodically to the auto races in the summer. One time I went with Kenny, from Shelby, who owned an Oldsmobile that he kept so clean that you could fry eggs on the manifold. After the races were over we were driving home when a new Thunderbird tried to pass us. Kenny speeded up and soon we were going 120mph side by side, going down a fairly long straightaway. Eventually Kenny slowed down to let the car pass.

Another football player, Frank, who had trained with Bill and I using our weight set had been taking piano lessons for several years. He asked if I played chess and when I said no, he told me that he would teach me. When I went to his house I asked him to play the piano and he was very accomplished. He told me that he would like to become a concert pianist but he ended up becoming a lawyer. I spent a few Sunday afternoons at his house playing some chess but I enjoyed hearing him play the piano more than the chess.

I was in chemistry class in 1956 when the Soviets launched sputnik that fall. From that time on all that we were interested in was making rocket fuel. We kept mixing different ratios of the chemical components.

One spring day our teacher was called to the principal's office just before lunch break. While he was out of class, we stuffed a 10 inch pipe, which someone had brought to class, with our newest concoction of rocked fuel. We capped one end, and attached the nozzle of the lab faucet to the other.

During lunch period, a group of students went outside the school building, just outside of the chemistry lab window, to light the wick that was trailing from the nozzle. I suggested that we take it to the middle of the baseball diamond to do this, but the wiz kids would not heed my advice, therefore, I did not go outside with them. Only by God's grace, no one was hurt. When that fuel lit, the nozzle exploded, going nearly a foot deep into the ground. The pipe split going straight up several thousand feet into the sky missing the school building. The sound was like a stick of dynamite being lit.

Immediately, we could hear the sound of the local police chief driving his cruiser to the school. I am sure a major discussion involving the police chief, the school administrator, and our instructor took place, but our instructor never really reprimanded us.

After that, we toned things down, but continued mixing various mixtures of fuel and tested it using wooden spools attached with string to the lab faucets. That is all that I remember from an entire year of chemistry. If you would like to read about a much better experience, which some other students enjoyed while making rockets, I would suggest reading: "Rocket Boys" by Homer Hickam, Jr.

I broke my collar bone during the last football game of my junior year. It happened in the second quarter when I tripped over one of our own players. I did not say a word to anyone and continued to play the rest of the game. I went to bed that night with some pain and planned to see a doctor in the morning. When I woke up, I could not get up, and began inching myself over to the edge of the bed to fall on the floor. I then managed to raise my good arm up to the bed and lift myself up.

I walked to the doctor's office and he was able to see me. After examining me, he confirmed that I had indeed broken my collar bone, but everything seemed to be in place. Therefore, he strapped me in a brace and told me to return in two weeks.

I had two follow up visits with him and after the first visit, I made sure that I would be his last patient of the day. I enjoyed my visits with Dr. Faust very much and we discussed many things long into the night. He told me many things including what medical school was like. He also told me about a book he had read while he was in medical school that was about a meeting of world leaders in which future events were discussed. He could not remember the name of it, but I remember our discussion and I have always been curious which book it might have been.

I had a classmate Daryl, who was on the track team with me. He kept hitting his shin on the crossbar when he would be high jumping. He developed a lump on that shin bone and had to have surgery. The wound would not heal, so the doctor put a cast on his leg and began treating it with maggot therapy. It caused a very foul odor.

That wound eventually turned into osteomyelitis, and he would miss school for weeks at a time. I would take homework to him and we would play with his train set. He never was able to run track again. His mother was a Methodist Sunday school teacher and the more Daryl studied the more convinced he was that he was an atheist.

My grandmother had developed cancer and had a terrible battle with it. I continued to bury myself with activities and accepted the offer to help out with janitorial work at the high school.

The village had a town basketball team and I would open the school to let the teams in to play one or two nights a week. I saw some very good basketball games. When the games were over, I would sweep the gym and clean up. I would sometimes break out a trumpet and do my best to play even though it was a lost cause.

One of the resources that we used in addition to the textbook for our sciences was a series of workbook/lab manuals titled Discovery Problems in Chemistry, Earth Science, Biology, and Physics. One spring our teacher stopped the class for a moment to order those materials for the next school year from the representative that had called on him. I thought to myself that would be an interesting job to have.

The launching of Sputnik had caused much discussion and although not expressed, I suspect apprehension about world events. My classmate Ted and I must have had a conversation about the event and apparently we discussed not having Bibles. We went to a bookstore in Mansfield where each of us purchased a copy, however, we never discussed if we had read anything from them.

It was August 20, 1957 when I began my last season of high school football. I loaded up with many classes, as usual, even though I needed only the government class to graduate. My grandmother's health was declining rapidly and I was thinking more and more about what I would do after graduation.

My grandfather had gone to Atlanta where he was superintendent of construction for the new WSB Atlanta television building named: "White Columns." When Christmas break arrived I took the bus to Atlanta to see him. While I was there we made a trip to Stone Mountain and I purchased a paperweight that I still use.

When I returned to school I did not have much enthusiasm. In addition to my grandmother's condition my mother's father was placed in a nursing facility and it was obvious that mother would soon be going for another hospitalization

On top of that I did another stupid thing. I had gone out for the senior play and again had the lead part. After three practices I quit! My friend Jim stepped in for me and did a great job.

I followed that up with an action that I am also not proud of. We had gone to Cedar Point and while there I found a billfold that had very little or no cash but did have a driver's license in it that I failed to return!

I believe that in most circumstances when we do wrong deeds it affects the one who has done them more than those affected. Even though I have confessed them to the Lord every time I go through the county that that person was from I am reminded of what I did.

One or both of the parents of the wife of the milkman I was working for had begun to experience severe health problems. George asked me if there was any way I could help him out during the week. I don't know if George had talked to the superintendant about my doing so or not but by the end of my senior year I had missed 31 days of school. I passed all my classes is spite of missing all that time. I had a gracious neighbor that understood what I was doing and he never said a word to me about it.

The usual senior class trip to Washington D.C. was scheduled and students were required to contribute to the expense. We were down to the last week of our final fund raising projects and I had done nothing. Magazine Subscription Sales was the project, and I forced myself to do it.

By the end of the week, I had made the required amount that we were expected to contribute, thanks to the Lord's help.

The senior prom was planned for the year end and I asked a girl from Willard to attend with me.

The night before the prom George called me and asked me to come to their home. When I arrived, he and his wife gave me a new watch, a cash gift, the keys to their new car, and told me to have a good time! He said I will see you in the morning.

Carole and I had a good time at the prom and when I took her home she asked me to come in even though it was well past midnight. We ended up talking to 5:30 am and I rushed home, changed clothes, and arrived just in time to help George load the milk truck. I was able to lie down on the ice on top of the milk crates to sleep a little between villages.

Graduation arrived, and my grandmother had willed herself to live to see me graduate. The nurse, who granddad had hired, along with his help managed to get her to the occasion in a wheelchair.

It had been decided by the state of Ohio or others to consolidate our rival school from Shiloh with Plymouth beginning in the fall. Arrangements had been made to combine the two senior classes for their trip to the capitol.

It turned out to be a very interesting trip. Since I was the secretary of our class I was privileged to ride in a limousine with the beautiful secretary from Shiloh along with two chaperones to our side trips while in D.C.

One evening, a group of us were in a fairly large room after returning from dinner with no chaperones. I did not participate, but a wrestling match began about eleven or twelve o'clock. It went on for at least an hour and was getting very loud. Participants were picking each other up over their heads and slamming one or the other to the floor. A very loud knock on the door was heard, and when it was opened, there stood the bellman, and in a pleading voice told us to stop as the chandelier below our room was swinging so hard that the lady in the room was afraid that it would fall! I had a great trip and saw many things of interest.

When I got off the train from the trip back and said my goodbyes it was "now what?" I thought about joining the Navy or perhaps the Air Force but I really did not want to leave until my grandmother had passed on.

Sometime, the spring of my senior year, I was reading the paper and saw a very elaborate advertisement for a shaving kit. I thought that it would be nice to have one, but was not sure if I would ever use it. I was hoping to get a job where I had very little contact with others.

When I returned from the trip, I was at the house when the postman came with the mail. It was Carol's father and he handed me a beautifully wrapped, pale blue carton with a bright yellow ribbon around it, and told me their family wanted to give me a graduation gift. I thanked him, and told him how much I appreciated them. We talked for a few minutes and he went on with his duties.

I took the gift into the house, carefully untied the ribbon, and removed the paper not knowing what to expect. Inside the carton was the exact shaving kit, which I had seen advertised in the paper earlier that spring! I thought: "how appropriate," as I probably would not be seeing that family, or many others that I had known, for a long time."

Continue with me as I tell you about the amazing and incredible journey of well over two million miles that I have traveled since receiving that wonderful gift.

The Encounter

In all thy ways acknowledge him and he shall direct thy ways.

Proverbs 3:6

The summer after graduation from high school was a very unsettling time in my life. My grandfather had returned home to spend the last days of my grandmother's life with her. I don't remember having one date with a girl and most of my friends were involved with their girlfriends or preparing to go to college.

Jim and I went to a dance in Willard one night and since I no longer was in school, I indulged in some beer. We had several cans of beer before starting for home. We were talking while Jim was driving and the car was weaving slightly as he drove. A patrolman noticed and stopped us. He detected the alcohol on Jim's breath, and pointed to me and said: "You better drive." I thought: "No, I am more unfit to drive than Jim!" When I opened the door, there was a deep ditch to step into, but I managed to step down into it, and held onto the car as I made my way to the back of it and climbed out of the ditch. I made it to the door and got in behind the steering wheel. I waited until the patrolman left before driving us home.

The patrolman did not give Jim a ticket or even lecture us. He did watch me pull away from the ditch to let Jim get in before he drove away.

I was walking up town later that summer and Daryl drove by and stopped. He had another classmate with him whose name was Pat. He asked me to join them and she slid over to the middle of the seat as I got in. My foot hit something on the floor when I got in and I reached down to see what it was. I saw that it was a pair of six pack cartons of beer. They told me they were headed someplace to sit, drink the beer, and talk. It sounded like a good idea to me.

I don't know where we went, but as we began talking it was obvious that all of us were somewhat unsure what we wanted to do in life. We drank and talked for several hours and when we finished the beer, Daryl drove Pat home. I'm not sure if she even went into her home. She may have slept on the front porch and I think that was the last time I saw her.

Daryl told me that he had received an Ohio Brass Company scholarship to attend college. He told me that he planned to go to The Ohio State branch that would begin having classes at Mansfield Senior High School in the fall. He asked me if I would be interested in enrolling in a few classes and commuting with him when classes began. I told him that I definitely would.

By the time he dropped me off at my grandfather's home where mother was staying, it was nearly dawn. As I was walking to the front door I became aware that I was not feeling well. I began to regurgitate in a very loud manner. Mother woke up and came out to the porch and asked: "What's the matter with you?" I replied: "Little boy had big night and not to worry about it." She went back into the house and nothing more was said.

Daryl had enrolled in one or two science classes in addition to the required English course. I was not sure what I wanted to do, but I had an interest in architecture, therefore, I enrolled in an engineering drawing course along with a psychology course and the required English course. Our classes were held on the same evenings and we were able to commute as planned.

On the first evening, all of the students were seated and waiting for our English instructor to arrive. He walked into the classroom, introduced himself, walked directly to the chalkboard, and wrote the word "doubt" on the board and said: "Start writing." At the end of class he gathered the papers and said: "See you next week."

There were twenty or more students in that class and five of them had been valedictorians! When the papers were returned the following week, he had assigned two students C grades, three a D and failed the rest. Some of the students were in tears because they had never received such a low grade. I felt grateful to have received a D, as I probably had the lowest GPA in the class.

That class continued in the same way all fall. No comments were shown on the papers and very little discussion of anything. I have to give him some credit because I believe my writing improved as a result of that experience.

I enjoyed the psychology class but I soon learned that architecture was not my suit. I had much trouble visualizing interior structures.

It began snowing very heavy the last part of November that year and my grandmother's death was near. She called each of us into her room a couple of days before she died and gave each a booklet titled "Personal Bible Verses of "Comfort, Assurance, and Salvation." She died Thanksgiving week and eight to ten inches of snow were on the ground when she was buried.

A few days after the funeral service my grandfather left for Oklahoma to begin a new construction project. I resumed commuting to college with Daryl and when the quarter ended he asked if I would be continuing the second quarter. I told him that I did not have the resources. and would not be attending classes for the second quarter. He told me that he had received scholarship money, and would loan me funds to do so. After much discussion, I agreed to accept his offer and I enrolled for the quarter.

It continued to snow for the next few weeks and suddenly turned to rain about mid December. This resulted in severe flooding over northern Ohio. Classed had concluded, and a week or ten days afterward I was walking across the street, heading for the library in a pouring down rain when the encounter took place.

The wind was blowing very hard and I heard someone calling my name from a car I did not recognize. I walked to the car to see who it was, and I saw my former scout master sitting behind the steering wheel. I had not seen him in several years as he and his family had moved to Mansfield. He told me that he had been detoured through Plymouth on his way home from Elyria, because of the flooding.

He asked how I was doing, and I told him that I had completed a quarter of college and was enrolled for the second quarter but I was having a hard time getting a job since I did not have a car.

We continued to talk while I was standing beside his car in the pouring rain. He told me that he could put me to work in Elyria after New Years' Day, but he did not think I should drop out of college. I asked what I would be doing and he told me that I would be using a jack hammer to repair holes in the road which the gas company dug to replace gas lines. I told him that I had never worked with a jack hammer and he told me that he would show me how. He told me that it was not complicated work, but was not easy work. I thought about it for a minute and told him I would like to do it. He questioned me again about dropping out of college, and I told him that it was more important for me to have a job.

I told him I did not have a way to get to Elyria and he told me that he would have his foreman pick me up early the morning after New Year's Day. He also told me to be sure I had very warm clothes to work in because I would be out all day.

I did not know what I was getting myself into, but it was time to move on. I purchased two pair of coveralls and packed a small suitcase. I also packed the shaving kit which I have continued to use since the day that that it was packed.

I called Daryl and told him that I would not be commuting with him for the second quarter, and that I would return the money he had loaned me after I had received my first check.

I don't remember seeing Daryl again until my sister's high school graduation. He told me that he had about six months to live and he still claimed to be an atheist. I prayed for him many times and cling to the hope that his mother had led him to the Lord when he was young. He also died in November. His death, along with my mother entering the hospital, and my grandmother's death have contributed to some tough times for me during the holiday season.

The Vision

Commit thy way unto the Lord; trust also in him, and he shall bring it to pass.
Psalms 37:5

Howie, my foreman arrived promptly at the designated time to pick me up for the ride to Elyria on that very cold, blustery first morning in January 1959. We soon found commonalty and were discussing our high school football careers. He had played for Mansfield Senior High during the early 1940's. He was married and his wife was a nurse.

We arrived in Elyria where he took me to a rooming house and showed me to my room. Several other workers were staying and we each had a separate bedroom but we shared the same bathroom on the second floor. The owner of the rooming house was a widow lady and the rent was seven dollars per week. Meals were not available but there was a restaurant not far away.

We proceeded to the construction office and I was introduced to Kenny, a man probably in his early 40's with whom I would be working. Kenny drove a dump truck and I was given a compressor truck to drive. After checking the oil and gasoline, we drove to the job site which was on the main east/west road going through the city.

We were going west and Kenny slowed down and went slowly over a large hole that had been filled in with the dirt that had been excavated by the gas company. I stopped the compressor truck behind the hole. We then placed cones along the sides of the trucks and directly behind the compressor truck to block off the work area.

My former scout master drove up, and we walked back to the compressor truck. He showed me how to start the compressor and attach the hose to the jack hammer. He also showed me how to insert the bits and which one to use for outlining a hole and which one to use for breaking up concrete. He carried the jack hammer to the hole and explained how to use it to form an outline around the hole.

He explained to me how a road was constructed. A blacktop road normally has a concrete base with 4 inches of blacktop. Our job was to dig a hole about one foot larger than the original hole and one foot deep. This would leave a ledge of undisturbed dirt around the original hole for the new concrete to rest on, so as to help prevent the repaired area from settling. It took less than two minutes to show me what I would be doing and he wished me well and left.

We were expected to dig eight hundred square feet a day. Our foreman would come by several times a day and when we were finished, he would determine how much concrete to order to fill all the holes to within four inches of the top.

Kenny and I had a good day. I learned much. The jack hammer weighed ninety-five pounds and the bit was driven by two hundred pounds of air pressure. The day was brutally cold and the wind was blowing very hard. I was ready to get in the truck for lunch and was certainly ready to rest when we finished.

Kenny was not staying at the rooming house. He may have been commuting from his home in Ashland. That evening I met another foreman Danny, who was staying with us at the rooming house. I had met his twin brother while attending classes in Mansfield. He had been in the engineering drawing class and I am quite sure he became an architect.

I also met a couple of former military men. Dutch was a former naval corpsman and the other had been in the army. There were several two man crews working in the Lorain, Elyria, and Cleveland areas. I would generally eat several times a week with the group living in the rooming house.

Occasionally, after the evening meal I would go with my co workers to a bar. The philosophy of the single men in particular, was to work hard, drink hard, and play hard. Initially, I did not participate in the drinking except for a coke but it was not long before I could drink with the best of them.

We were eating our evening meal one night when I saw a couple that I thought I had met in Plymouth many years ago. I started talking with them and I had indeed met them. They told me they were taking dancing lessons in Lorain and invited me to go with them some night. By that time I was concerned about how much I had been drinking each week and I accepted their invitation.

The following week they picked me up and we went to Arthur Murray's in Lorain. It was expensive but not nearly as much as I was spending on my drinking habit. I went with them for five or six weeks and I had a good time.

Spring had finally arrived and the group from the rooming house along with some other workers joined a fast pitch softball league. It was a very competitive league and we played twice a week. The pitching was outstanding. I played four years of high school baseball and this was a new experience. I think I had only two hits for the summer!

One evening after a ball game we went to a bar that was inside a log cabin. We entered and sat down at a round table with six chairs. I was trying to curb my drinking habit and when I didn't order anything Danny asked me: "Why?" I told him that it was becoming too expensive.

He told me that he would pay for anything that I wanted to drink. I could not resist the offer and began to drink five or six water glasses of straight vodka. I immediately became very sick and stood up to go outside and regurgitate. On my way to the door I knocked over several chairs and a table while the bar maid was hitting me with her broom as I made my exit.

I made it to the back of the building where I expelled all I had drunk. It was a good thing or I probably would have died of alcohol poisoning. I went to work the next morning as though nothing had happened.

My drinking had become a serious problem for me. It did not affect my work and I drank only during the week but I had acquired a real taste for straight whisky. It did not make me sick. I began to think about how I was going to leave the area and start over.

There was a young man about my age that had started working with us that spring, and he told me that he planned to try to get work on an ore boat that plied the great lakes. He told me that he would be going to Cleveland to apply for his seaman's card and I asked to go with him. He told me that I may not be able to get one because of my poor vision. He was not sure what the requirements were for galley work. I did not want to work in the galley but I was getting anxious to get away.

We went to Cleveland and he was able to get his card, however, my application was declined due to vision problems. He left the company a week or two after receiving his seaman's card and I have not had contact with him since he left.

I continued working, drinking, and playing softball. It was now July and I had not saved one dime. I had purchased a small desk with small round legs that unscrewed for easy transportation. I also purchased a folding chair to go with it. With the exception of a few books, that was my major purchase while I was in Elyria.

My room expense was seven dollars a week and I was making two hundred plus a week and had virtually spent all on drink! I had to leave. My life had become drinking and listening to Andy Williams sing: "Lonely Street" on the radio.

There was a policeman's ball scheduled for the last part of July and we had been invited to attend. I agreed to go with the rest of the group. When we arrived, the very large facility was nearly full. We split up, and after asking if I could join them, I sat down with a few other people that I did not know.

I presume we introduced ourselves but I don't remember doing so. We purchased a fifth of whiskey to go with whatever there was to eat. By the end of the evening I had drunk nearly a fifth of whiskey by myself and was still able to walk quite well. I had also eaten quite a lot over the fours that we were there.

When I got up the next morning I was totally disgusted with myself for having drunk all that whiskey. I was not ill and went to work as usual.

I don't remember who I was working with that day. By the time we arrived at the work site, it was a beautiful sun shinny day with not a cloud in the blue sky. As I was working, I kept noticing a few cars driving by with their windows closed. Air conditioned cars were very rare at that time.

I continued to work and watch cars go by and I became very angry with myself. I raised that ninety-five pound jack hammer with the pointed bit over my head and slammed it to the concrete. Instead of hitting the concrete, I hit the large toe of my left foot dead center and had felt two pumps of that jack hammer hit before I lifted it from my toe.

Even though I had on steel toed shoes the pain was unbelievable.

I immediately screamed out to the good Lord and said: "Lord, I hate myself. I was not raised this way. I want three things in life. I want a wife that is faithful, a college education, and a job like one of those people riding around in air conditioned cars."

Immediately, I saw a vision of a very bright light with two hands pointing down to a full round table and another half table with people sitting on chairs. It was obviously part of a large audience and a question was asked of me: "If I give it to you, will you tell these?"

I was stunned. I had just turned nineteen years old a few weeks earlier and the last thing I wanted was to be a public speaker. I weighed that question for what seemed to be a full minute. If I answered no I would continue on as a drunk. I finally realized that if the Lord called me to do it, he would help me, and I told him that I would. When I answered him the vision I had seen left.

I did not say a word about the vision I had seen but my desire for alcohol was gone. A few days later a representative from Bliss Business College in Columbus was at the door holding a reply card from me and wanted to talk to me. Apparently, I had sent a request to them but could not recall doing it. After hearing what he had to say, I enrolled for the fall quarter.

I gave my two week's notice and saved my last two paychecks. I had made over twenty-five hundred dollars and only had four hundred left.

On a beautiful Saturday morning I packed my small suitcase, took the legs off the desk top, and folded my chair. I picked everything up and walked to state route 57 and began hitch hiking to Columbus. It was not too long before a lady in a pick-up truck stopped for me and drove me to where she was turning to go to her house. I made it to Columbus sometime that evening.

The Blind Date

Delight thyself also in the Lord; and he shall give you the desires of thine heart.
                                          Psalms 37:4

I arrived in Columbus with enough money to pay for my first quarter tuition and a month's room rent. I was directed to Mrs. Root's party home where I would be staying with several other students. Austerity was the name of the game as I had no job.

As time passed I became quite concerned and the college job placement official directed me to a nursing home for employment. I worked for one hour and could not handle being around so many ill people. I had watched my grandmother's health decline over a five year period while she was fighting cancer. I went to the supervisor and told her that I was leaving and that I did not expect to be paid for the hour I was there.

There were two large conventions being held that fall in Columbus and Mrs. Root's catering service had contracted to serve the two main meals for the events. I was one of the students hired to help with that task. I was assigned to help make coffee and help with serving the meals. It was quite a job as there were over 5000 people in attendance for each meal.

Each morning as we walked to class, we passed the Navy recruiting office and I would say to my friend Larry: "Should I join the Navy for three square meals a day or go to class?" He would always reply: "Another day of school won't hurt you."

I became more acquainted with some of my classmates and I decided to move across the street to another rooming house where they were living. One beautiful summer day Larry and I went swimming at Buckeye Lake east of Columbus. I foolishly wore my glasses into the water and lost them when I was hit by an unexpected small wave while swimming. Larry and I spent over a half hour looking for them, but did not find them. Maybe a fish needed glasses.

Business College was going very well and I enjoyed it. I acquired more practical business knowledge in just one quarter than I did from any two quarters of liberal arts college courses. We attended classes from 7:00am until 12:50pm. I was getting very concerned about a job and was very relieved when the job placement official sent me to Highlights for Children.

When I arrived at 1:00pm, I was taken to a table and shown a stack of requests for information on teaching your child to talk. I would stuff envelopes with the information requested and when that task was completed I was taught how to operate an addressograph machine. That machine made labels to be used by the printer to mail the magazines to subscribers.

At the end of the day I was assigned various janitorial duties to be completed before leaving. I enjoyed the work and within a short period of time I began working in the accounting department several hours each day. Soon I was working full time in accounting.

Highlights for Children was in the process of having a new facility built several miles away and expected to move into it the spring of 1960. Since I was already working full time in the accounting department, I decided not to enroll for spring quarter at Bliss.

I was speaking with a classmate from Tiffin a few days before the first quarter ended, and she told me that she would like to go to a communion service being held at a nearby Methodist church but she had no one to go with. I told her that I would accompany her as it had been a long time since I had been in church. I went with her and we never saw each other again.

I was working late one evening when the president of Highlights came in and asked what I was doing there so late. I told him that I was working on a project that I wanted to complete before morning. He worked about a half hour and came to where I was working and asked where I lived. I told him and he insisted on driving me to the rooming house which was slightly more than a mile east of the office location. We had a wonderful conversation while he drove me home. He then had to drive to a western suburb to his home.

Spring arrived and Highlights moved to their new facility. I was still living on the east side of the city and began taking the city bus to work.

A short time after moving into the new facility an open house was held for anyone that wanted to see the new building. It was a major event at that time and busloads of people were transported to view the building and meet the president of Highlights and his father and mother who had founded the company. The mayor of Columbus attended along with many dignitaries.

I had the opportunity to meet Dr. Myers and his wife who founded Highlights for Children. They were elderly with very sharp minds and I enjoyed our conversation immensely.

I remained living at the rooming house for several months and continued to commute to work via the bus. I was learning more and more in my work and was assigned to help the auditors with their work. It was very good experience.

Meanwhile Bob, one of the students at Bliss, who was also staying at the rooming house, had a date with a former acquaintance of his who he had met several years previously at a church camp. She was now in nursing training at Mansfield General Hospital and she had insisted that he bring someone to go with her friend to make it a double date. He knew that I was from the Mansfield area and therefore asked me to go with him. Since I had not dated anyone since leaving Elyria I agreed to go with him.

Bob and I drove up to Mansfield on May 14, 1960 to meet the two nursing students, Beth and Marilyn. As we got into the car I introduced myself as "Ed" rather than my first name Larry. Marilyn was expecting to be going out with a "Larry" and was sure Bob had picked someone else to come with him. I went on to explain that my name was: "Larry Edward" and that I went through high school by "Ed." After graduating and filling out job applications which asked to fill in first name and middle initial, I decided to go by Larry to make things easier. All of my business associates know me by Larry and many others know me as Ed. Apparently one of my parents wanted an Ed and the other preferred Larry.

If I am not mistaken we went to dinner that evening and attended a movie before returning them to the dorm prior to their curfew. Things must have gone well because when we asked to see them the next day, they agreed to do so. It did not go so well with Beth and Bob and it was their last date. Marilyn and I continued to see each other and the following weekend, I began hitch hiking many times to Mansfield and returning to Columbus via bus.

Marilyn had made arrangements for me to stay in the home of a former classmate of hers while he was away to college. During that summer and fall I met many of Marilyn's relatives and introduced her to mine. She had two years left of nursing training before she could become a nurse. I decided to enroll at The Ohio State University and continue to work for Highlights.

There was a fellow from New York named "Stratis" who had leased a two bedroom apartment when he moved to Ohio. It was very close to the campus of Ohio State and he asked me if I would like to rent the extra bedroom from him to help with his expenses, and I accepted his offer immediately. Stratis had worked for Prentice Hall Publishing while in New York and had moved to Columbus to work for Highlights in the advertising department. Our arrangement worked out very well. I rode with him to work in the morning and walked to the campus several nights a week for class.

Things were going well. I was working, going to classes, and seeing Marilyn on the weekends. It was soon the holiday season and I had gone to inner city Columbus to do some shopping. While doing so I met the president of Highlights and his wife who were also shopping. We had a very nice visit and they told me that they would be flying to New York the next day to continue their shopping. Mrs. Myers had broken her leg while skiing out west in the spring and she was finally out of her cast. It was so good to see them so happy. They were very fine people and we wished each other a Merry Christmas and said our goodbyes.

I will never forget December 16, 1960. Jack, my supervisor and I were sitting at our desks when we were informed of a plane collision over New York City. Mr. and Mrs. Myers along with one or two others from the company had been on one of the planes. All were killed. It was a very somber Christmas that year.

I had enrolled in several courses for the winter quarter and was looking forward to resuming my routine. A few days after Christmas, I was returning to the apartment well after midnight. As I entered the door of that dark living room I was attacked by some kind of animal that had buried his claws in my side. When I finally found the light and turned it on, I was looking at a Siamese cat hanging on my side. I turned around very fast and the cat went flying to the floor. We had an instant hate for each other and it took me several minutes to reach the safety of my bedroom.

The next morning Stratis informed me that he had agreed to take care of the cat while the girl that he was seeing was gone for the weekend. I was relieved that the cat and I were through.

The one year lease that Stratis had signed for the apartment was coming to a close and he told me that he had decided to take a year off and travel. I also had been thinking about moving to Mansfield.

I still had a couple of weeks of classes left before the quarter ended, therefore, I rented a nearby room for two or three weeks. Stratis and I said our goodbyes and I heard from him only one time after he finished his travel time. He had returned to New York.

I began thinking about what I should do. I liked my job and yet I wanted to be closer to Marilyn. Construction work season was beginning again and although I was not looking forward to resuming that type of work, the compensation was substantially better than what I was making. After much deliberation and prayer, love won out and I called to see if I could return to my previous work. I was told yes but I would be working in Mansfield! How the Lord provided again.

It had been a little more than a year and a half since hitch hiking from Elyria to Columbus, but what an experience I had. I left Columbus April 1961.

The Provision

This is the day which the Lord hath made:
We will rejoice and be glad in it.
                                    Psalms 118:24

I arrived in Mansfield early April 1961 and rented a single bedroom apartment a couple of blocks away from the home of Marilyn's parents. I began working with that jack hammer again and even though I enjoyed working outside, I missed the accounting work in Columbus. However, I felt like I was doing what I should be doing.

After earning a couple of paychecks, my future father-in-law made arrangements for me to purchase my first automobile. It was a 1955 Chevy that had low mileage and was in excellent condition. I also began saving some of my earnings. This was a major change from my first construction work experience.

In May of that year Marilyn began experiencing some health problems. The first doctor accused her of being pregnant. She scheduled an appointment with another doctor and after examining her, he scheduled her for immediate surgery.

On the day of her surgery I met her parents at the hospital and we were quite concerned and did not know what to expect. After quite some time, the surgeon entered the room where we were waiting for the operation to be completed. Her parents and I stood up with me in the middle of them. He was still in his surgery gown and as he showed us the seven to eight pound ovarian cyst that he had removed from Marilyn, he asked me: "When are you are you kids planning to get married?" I told him that we planned to wait until Marilyn was through with her nurses' training. He replied: "If you want children, I would suggest that you get married before that and get at it." That was all he said, and turned and left the room.

Marilyn recovered quickly without any complications. We discussed what the doctor had told me and we began making plans for our marriage. I told her that I wanted to purchase a ring for her before formally proposing. We went to a jewelry store and she picked out the ring that she would like to have and I began making the payments for it.

We agreed that I would not resume college until her training was completed. I spent that summer working, playing softball on our church team, and fishing with my future father-in-law. I also began helping him with some accounting work during the month end closing of the books.

Fall arrived and I made the final payment on Marilyn's ring and I proposed in October. We set the wedding date for March 9, 1962.

I was transferred back to Elyria late October and began commuting rather than staying in a rooming house. On the very day in February that our wedding invitations were mailed, I arrived at the office in Elyria and was told that I was laid off from work!

I returned to Mansfield and began immediately to look for a job. Initially, I was trying to find work in accounting or similar work but had no success. My future father-in-law told me not to worry about it but to just keep hunting. The wedding would go on as planned.

I kept looking for work and by the Thursday before our Friday night wedding I had been to over 30 places and had taken numerous tests and still had not found a job. I was driving back from Shelby and I remembered that Daryl had received a scholarship from the Ohio Brass Company. I then realized that I had not contacted that company.

It was after lunch and I drove directly to the company and found the personnel office and asked the secretary if I may see the Personnel Director. He welcomed me into his office and I told him of my effort to find a job. I told him that I would prefer a job in the accounting department but that I would do anything because of getting married the following evening.

I will never forget Mr. Pollock. He was sitting in his chair not saying anything. He walked to the window in his office and stood there for another few minutes. He then turned to me and said: "Come with me."

We walked across the street to the shipping department and he introduced me to the foreman.

After speaking with him for a few minutes, he told me that he would make arrangements for me to see a doctor in the morning for a physical exam. He then told me that I was to report for work on Monday morning!

The Lord is good! He indeed provides for our needs. He may give us some of our wants, but not always as He knows what our future is.

I had rented another one bedroom apartment near the hospital where Marilyn had taken her training. The person who took me to see it told me that I probably would want to repaint it before moving in. I met her at the apartment to see it on the Monday before our wedding on Friday evening. As we entered, I could not believe my eyes.

The person who had rented it, painted everything including the metal window sills and metal doors with a solid blue water based paint. I don't remember if the ceiling was blue or not but I have never seen such a place. After doing all of that the person decided to not move in.

Marilyn's father helped me when he could, but I spent the entire week looking for a job and painting at night. In addition I moved furniture and other belongings from one apartment to the new one. By the time of the wedding I was totally exhausted.

I arrived at the church ten minutes or less before the wedding and I guess many people were relieved to see me. It had started to snow that evening and my father had trouble getting into his suit. All of the wedding party had arrived much earlier and were concerned also.

It was a beautiful wedding and there were many guests. My mother in law had baked the cake and it was a four tiered one with two or three side cakes. It also was beautiful. By the time the reception was over it was after 10:00pm. Several people helped our parents move gifts from the church to our apartment while Marilyn and I headed for Cleveland. There was over 4 inches of snow on the ground and we did not arrive at the hotel until after midnight.

Marilyn woke me up about 2:30 and said she was hungry and wanted to go to a restaurant. I thought she was testing me to see what I would do. She explained that she had not eaten anything at our reception and that she was starved. We dressed and went to a restaurant which was full of hung over people just ending their night out.

After eating, we went back to the hotel and slept a few hours before leaving for Niagara Falls. It continued to snow and by the time we reached Dunkirk, New York it was obvious we would not be going on to the falls. We ate and checked into a small motel.

Very early that Sunday morning the desk clerk pounded on the door and said he had a phone message for me and told me to come to the office. I thought that it was strange because we had not told anyone where we were. I went to the office and he told me that my wife had called and that I was to get home. I told him that my wife was in the room and that we did not live in New York. He did not know that another person had checked in after us and apologized profusely.

We had breakfast and started for home. A patrolman pulled us over and I asked what I had done. He said that he had a message that a car like ours had hit someone and left the scene of the accident. He was checking to be sure it was not our car he was looking for. After walking around our car, he told us to continue on our way.

The third incident occurred when we stopped for gas. Attendants pumped all gas in those days. After filling our tank, he walked back to the window and wished us a happy marriage. My best man Jim had put a note on the gas cap saying: "Just married."

We arrived at our apartment that evening and when we opened the door we were overwhelmed with the generosity of our friends and family. There were gifts everywhere. Our bed was covered with gifts. We began going through them and storing them where we could with our somewhat limited space. We were finally able to go to bed and Marilyn resumed her studies and I began my new Job.

When I arrived for work, the foreman took me to a packing bench and I began packing smaller parts for UPS shipment. I later learned how to pack many other parts for shipment. My co workers were very kind and taught me a lot. I enjoyed what I was doing but was getting anxious to return to college again for evening classes.

It was soon August and time for Marilyn's graduation from nurses' training. There were as I recall 55 graduates that received there three year diploma. During their years of study I had met many of them along with husbands or significant other. Their class was a special class as they were very close and have remained so since graduating.

In July I received notice to report to the draft board for a physical exam and tests to prepare me for the US Army. When I arrived there were over 30 of us and of course no women in those days. We were put on a bus to transport us from Norwalk to Cleveland. I was totally shocked at the number of recruits that were lacking in basic reading skills. Examiners were working with many of them individually to obtain the minimum score required for service.

While I had a strong desire to fulfill my military duty I did not want to go to the army. I was told that I should be expecting to be called in September. When I returned to Mansfield I went to our local Air National Guard unit to enquire about enlisting with them. I knew that the unit had been activated for the Berlin crisis. I met with the recruiter and he told me that deactivation would be taking place in August and that many guardsmen would be finished with their enlistment obligation and would be getting out. He told me to return the last half of August. I returned and was sworn in 29 August!

After graduating Marilyn continued to work at the hospital. Her state board tests to become a RN were scheduled for October. My basic training for the guard was also scheduled for October. We drove to Columbus together that fall and Marilyn was pregnant. She dropped me off at the base and returned to the hotel. Her tests began the following day. I boarded a plane for Texas that afternoon.

When we arrived at Lackland Air Force base training center we were assigned to our trainer. The first thing he said was:"You better shape up fast because you may be going to Cuba." The missile crisis had begun and no one knew what would be happening.

I found the physical training to be a piece of cake. My first football coach would have killed half of our squadron. The real challenge was a mental challenge as they tried to break everyone down so that orders would be unquestionably obeyed instantly. I would guess that 95% of the recruits in our squadron were college graduates, and many were working in their chosen professions. One afternoon a young officer was drilling us very intensely on the drill field. We had marched for over an hour straight when four or five guardsmen cracked and fell out of rank and walked to a nearby tree in tears.

During our training we were given demerits for various reasons like shoes not shined properly, items not displayed properly in our drawers, etc. No one escaped receiving at least one while training.

Joe Torrey, the former Yankee Manager was in one of the neighboring squadrons and he had a unique assignment. He has the most penetrating eyes of anyone I have seen. He would be sitting on a bench in the bottom of one of the barracks and recruits who had received a particular number of demerits would have to go and sit opposite Joe and stare at him. He could stare a hole through solid steel! I did not have to do this but went with a recruit who had to, just to see Joe.

When basic training was completed we went to see the Alamo and had a good steak dinner. It was good to see some of San Antonio other than the base.

I was assigned to supply school in Amarillo and boarded a bus for the long ride the second day after completing basic training. I arrived just before Thanksgiving weekend. School was very good and very intense. Six straight hours beginning at 6:00am and other duties assigned for the afternoons.

Two airmen from our squadron were selected as leaders. One was the grandson of a well known candle factory owner in New York. Every time I take communion I think of Michael.

During the Christmas holiday Michael and I went to stay in a hotel in Amarillo for one night. After checking in Michael proceeded to open a bottle of scotch and began drinking and polishing his shoes. I left and ended up having dinner with an Amarillo family that was very gracious to airmen not able to go home for the holidays. I don't remember how I was invited but I enjoyed a very fine meal. Many families were doing the same thing for servicemen. I was very remiss for not getting their names and sending a thank you card when I returned home.

When I returned to the hotel Michael's shoes must have had ten coats of polish on them as they glowed. His scotch was also gone. We returned to the base and resumed our training.

I sure learned about those Texas winds. My room was on the second floor of the barracks. The water in my shoe polish lid was frozen and the room directly across the hall was ninety degrees.

I was on guard duty one night watching B 52s take off. I could not believe how big they were. It was amazing that they were able to get off the ground.

Supply school ended and I headed home. After leaving the base the plane landed in Wichita before continuing to Chicago where I changed planes to go to Columbus. We landed in Columbus in a very heavy snow storm. I was dressed in Air Force blues and grabbed my heavy overcoat from my duffel bag. I hailed a cab and asked the driver to take me to the interchange of route 161 and interstate 71. By the time we arrived, there were four or five inched of snow all over and the wind was blowing very hard.

The cab driver tried to get me to check in at a hotel because it was after 1:00am and the weather was so poor. I told him that I had been gone for four months, that I was dressed warm, and that I would be fine. He drove slowly away as I walked down the entrance ramp to the interstate. The weather indeed was brutal.

Soon I saw a car approaching and it passed on by, probably having not seen me. Sometime later a semi truck passed by and continued up the highway. There was very little traffic and the weather was not getting any better. I was beginning to think that I was in for a very long night.

About twenty minutes later I saw another truck coming down the highway. The driver blinked his lights and brought his rig to a stop over a hundred yards pass me. I picked up that heavy duffel bag and started running toward the truck. By the time I reached it, I had barely enough strength to throw it up to the driver. It was probably 2:30am by this time.

We started talking and ironically he had left Amarillo not many hours before I did. As we continued to talk he asked where I was headed to. I told him Mansfield and he asked me where in Mansfield. I told him and he was very familiar with the city and he told me he would drop me at my front door.

We arrived at our apartment about 4:00am and the snow was still blowing like in a blizzard and falling as hard as ever. I thanked the driver and wished him well as he was continuing on to New York.

I did not have keys and stood on the walk not wanting to wake Marilyn but I was not going to stay outside. I walked to the door and knocked. My beautiful wife came to the door and as we embraced I could detect a major change in her body since we had said goodbye the previous fall. She was now about six months pregnant.

She had passed all five parts of her test and was now a registered nurse. She was still working at the hospital. I called the Ohio Brass Company that morning and was told to report for work on Monday morning.

When I arrived at work, I was told that the shipping department had been slow and that I would have to go to the foundry department. I went there and was put to work inspecting small parts called roof bolts. They were used in coal mines. I worked in that capacity for several weeks before returning to the shipping department. I saw those roof bolts in my sleep for many nights.

We began looking for a two bedroom apartment and found one just before our son, Jim, arrived.

When I returned from supply school I began attending training with the ANG one weekend a month. A week or two after Jim was born I went to Alpena, Michigan for my first summer camp with the guard. It was great duty and we had every other day off to allow training for all the members. I played golf with one of the other airmen and after playing we went to the beach where I experienced the worst sunburn in my life.

Soon after returning from summer camp we resumed our monthly meetings. I was walking from the supply building down to the mess hall for lunch and there was a second lieutenant walking up to the supply building. I saluted him and he returned the salute. I knew who he was but had never met him. I instantly thought that he would be a commanding officer one day. His salute had portrayed himself as not cocky but of absolute confidence in himself.

He ended up becoming commander of the base and went on to be commander of the state of Ohio Air National Guard. I had the opportunity of telling him of that experience and what I had thought when it happened many years ago. He died a couple years later. I had absolute respect for him and his family which I became acquainted with at our former neighbor's holiday parties.

Soon after Jim was born Marilyn returned to the hospital to work. I resumed attending classes at Ashland College and my dear mother-in-law would baby sit for us as we juggled our schedules. I would go to class two evenings a week and after class would pick up Jim and put him to bed. It was a long haul but I was determined to earn a degree with a major in accounting.

Marilyn became pregnant soon after Jim was born and I thought that doctor was crazy. I returned home from college one evening and a new television was sitting on a stand. Marilyn told me her father had brought it over earlier that evening. He also told her we needed something else to do!

The spring of 1964 we began apartment hunting again and we moved into a half double just before our daughter, Tamara arrived less than thirteen months after Jim was born.

Marilyn continued to work at the hospital and I continued working in the shipping department. My mother-in-law was now babysitting with two young children while I attended classes two nights a week. I was making progress with my accounting education.

About mid April 1965, the plant manager came to the shipping department and asked to see me. I had not met him and had no idea why he wanted to meet with me. He told me that he and others were aware that I had been attending college and he wanted to offer me a better job. He escorted me to the general office building and took me to meet Jack, who was the son of the personnel manager. Jack explained the job to me and I gladly accepted it, and became a sales correspondent the following day.

At that time several utility companies were involved with building those large transmission lines across the country. The Ohio Brass Company was a major manufacturer of hardware components and porcelain insulators for that project. My job as a sales correspondent was handling phone inquiries from purchasing agents and our district managers requesting information about particular orders. After our phone discussions I would dictate letters confirming what we had discussed.

It was a demanding job and many times I would return to work after attending class and dictate letters for several hours. As demanding as the job was, I liked what I was doing and was gaining valuable experience in how to converse with sometimes very upset individuals. You have never been chewed out until you have experienced a call similar to one from a purchasing agent with construction crews shut down and paying heavy fines because product did not arrive as promised.

One evening Jack and I worked at his home until 1:30am or 2:00am scheduling shipments for an overwhelming number of orders. Deliveries were estimated to be two to three years away. There were several manufacturers of materials and I suspect orders were placed with all of them at times in hope of getting an earlier delivery.

I worked in that department for several years and enjoyed every minute of it. There was a sales engineer, Al, who was over all the sales correspondents and he was especially encouraging to me about my college work. Another sales engineer, Joe, liked to play golf and I would occasionally play with his group. He would travel to Los Angeles several times a year on business and his eyes would water for days because of the smog in that city.

In early 1969 a real estate broker who was a member of our church asked me if I would be interested in purchasing a home if he could find one with no money down and a payment of what we were paying for rent. I told him of course I would be interested in doing so.

It was not long before he found a home and we went to see it and began the purchasing process. I asked Al if he would write a letter of recommendation for me to get our loan. He wrote a letter that stunned me. He said nothing that was untrue but seeing it in writing was unbelievable. I told Al that someday I would sell that recommendation meaning that I would use it to obtain another job after completing college. I still have that letter. His response was: "You deserved it."

We moved into that house on July 4, 1969 in a pouring down rainstorm.

My service in the guard had gone well. I took several military courses and rank was open above me. This allowed me to obtain the rank of staff sergeant in a relatively short period of time.

There was An ANG bowling tournament scheduled to be held in New Orleans in February 1968. I applied to go and was accepted. I did not have bowling equipment and my wife purchased a bowling ball for me. I purchased a bag and shoes from another sales engineer.

We left Columbus on a beautiful cloudless day on a large plane used for refueling other aircraft.

The plane quickly reached cruising altitude and I mustered up the courage to walk out on the glass bottom and lay down to look at all the geography below. I was able to see Lake Erie, The Ohio River, and the junction of the Mississippi River with the Ohio River in one view. It was a beautiful sight.

When we landed, airmen from New Orleans handed each of us a key chain with a knife, nail file, and a small screw driver with a bottle opener folded into it. It was also engraved to celebrate the event. I am still carrying that keychain over 47 years later and have opened thousands of cartons since I received it.

I had a very good time while there. I lasted longer in the tournament than I expected and I was able to have dinner in the French Quarter with a district manager and his wife. I also went on a river boat excursion and that captain talked continuously for over four hours telling us about various places as we passed by. He talked not only about the history but also about the oil industry and the miles of pipe being laid on the ocean floor.

Before I was to get out of the guard the supply officer called me into his office and asked me if I would be interested in going to officer candidate school. My wife and I talked it over and I decided not to proceed with it. Our unit had briefly been activated for the Cleveland riots and I was still taking courses at college. I told the officer of my decision and was discharged in August 1968. I enjoyed my guard duty and it certainly contributed to my development.

A few months prior to moving into our home an opening occurred in the marketing department of Ohio Brass and I decided to apply for the position. As a result of my experience in the sales department I was beginning to think about sales work. I thought the position in marketing would be a nice fit between my sales correspondence work and my accounting education.

I transferred into the marketing department just prior to moving into our home in 1969. It turned into a good move for me. Our manager was highly competent and taught me many things about the nuts and bolts of analyzing various markets. My title was marketing analyst. I did some very detailed market studies during my time in that department.

A few weeks after moving into our home we met our neighbors who lived directly behind us. Carl and Shirley and their children had moved from Horseheads, New York to Lexington several months to a year ahead of us. Carl was with a small publishing company that published workbook/lab manuals and a couple of health texts used at the middle school/junior high level and the high school. Carl and I along with another neighbor, Chuck, began playing ping pong in our basement. We soon developed a great friendship. Chuck was also involved in sales work and I enjoyed hearing about their experiences.

About that time a number of families including ours left a church with their blessing to form a new church in Lexington. We called a pastor who had just completed seminary. Marilyn and I became very good friends with him and his wife. Soon Pastor

Terry and I began early morning jogs around our development. We also along with several other men began a Boys Brigade program for the young men from our church and others who wanted to attend. It was very rewarding.

Marilyn and I had been married for over seven years and had never gone away for a very long vacation. I happened to mention this to my manager's secretary and she told me that she and her husband owned a cottage in Michigan. I loved Michigan and had never been farther north than Ludington. She told me that the cabin was on a beautiful lake in the town of Beulah.

We rented that cottage and I will never forget that beautiful drive down the hill from Benzonia overlooking that clear blue lake on the way to Beulah. It is a lake nearly seven miles long and about two miles wide at its' greatest width. It became my favorite vacation spot and we have been there many times.

The first time we were there Neil Armstrong was stepping out of his space capsule to the moon's surface. Our two children were five and six years old and I had them on the shore of the lake and pointed to that beautiful full moon and told them to watch closely to see him walk on the moon.

We returned from that vacation very refreshed. Both Marilyn and I returned to work and I began attending classes once more.

Late that fall a member of our church who was an insurance agent contacted me to go over our program. He was a few years older than I was and I asked if he would like to join the pastor and myself for our early morning jaunts. He replied: "Are you kidding, I wouldn't do that for any reason in the world." I asked why and he responded: "both of your wives are pregnant!" I had not paid any attention but both were in fact due in May.

Our pastor was from Altoona, Pennsylvania and he had made arrangements for several men to take a group of boys from our Brigade program to Trough Creek state park for a two camping trip in May. We left the second week of May to take eight or ten boys on that trip to the chagrin of our mothers-in-law. I was driving a 1967 Camaro and followed him in his Volkswagon. Another driver was with us, but I forget the details.

Raystown Lake dam was being built at that time and he drove through on the lake bottom to reach the park. We took the boys to Penns Cave and Horseshoe Curve. We enjoyed the trip and returned to Lexington in time to be home with our wives when they gave birth. My wife had another daughter and his wife had another son.

Our friends, Carl and Shirley and their family moved back to New York in June and another young couple moved into the house directly across the street from ours. We introduced ourselves and we became very close friends.

We did many things together. We made a trip to Dalton, Georgia to purchase carpet for our homes. Terry and I did a decent job of laying it without any wrinkles.

He and his wife, Toni, helped me panel our basement. I helped him install a fireplace in their basement. All was going well until we were connecting the steel insulated chimney pipes. I was on their roof and had just attached the last two pipes when I heard a loud crash.

Toni came from their bedroom to see Terry's feet hanging down from their living room ceiling!

One year Terry purchased a small pool table and he called me to help him move it from the garage to the basement. After much struggle it was very apparent that we would not be able to move it inside and make the turn to get it to the stairs leading to the basement. We were standing in his garage thinking how we should proceed.

Another neighbor, Bill, was driving by the house and saw us in the garage. He asked what we were doing and when we told him, he asked for Terry's saber saw. He walked to the garage wall and immediately cut a hole in the wall large enough for us to pass the pool table through to the stairway. We assembled the table and began playing pool. A half hour went by and we were still playing as Toni drove in to the garage looking through the opening in the wall to see us playing pool.

Many new young families were moving to Lexington and our church was growing. I continued to help the pastor with Boys Brigade. I also helped with mowing the church lawn.

Terry and I also began playing golf and we became involved with little league ball with our boys. Terry became a sales representative for the company he was working for and I listened to his sales experiences.

I continued to work in the marketing department and was taking a speech course in college. While doing this, my father- in- law asked me one Sunday evening what I was doing for the next three weekends. I told him I had nothing planned and he said: "Good." I have enrolled both of us in the Dale Carnegie sales and management courses. It was very good training for me.

About that same time I met a manager for LaSalle extension courses and he asked me if I would be interested in doing some part time sales work. I accepted the offer and began selling courses in the evening. It gave me some good sales experience.

In August 1972, Marilyn made arrangements for us to visit her cousin Norma and her family who lived in New London, Connecticut. We called Carl and Shirley and made arrangements to spend a night or two with them before continuing on to New London. We had not seen them since they had moved back to New York and we had a wonderful time.

Carl had made plans for us to play golf with a friend of his who was in the area and was on his way back to Arizona. We met at the golf course and played nine holes and went to the clubhouse for lunch. As we talked, Bob told us he was working for Highlights for Children. It had been over 10 years since I had worked for Highlights and Bob and I had a good conversation about the company.

Carl and Bob had talked for over an hour and as I listened to them discuss their experiences, as sales representatives, I made up my mind to seriously begin to look for a sales job when we returned home. I interrupted their conversation to announce my decision. I told them that I had been considering sales work and that after listening to them talk, I was giving myself six months to find a sales job.

We stayed with Carl and Shirley that night and after breakfast in the morning we continued our trip to Norma's home. We arrived that evening and she had prepared Lobster Bisque for dinner. She and her husband Jack still had their youngest child John, who was about ten or twelve years' of age, living with them. After everyone had eaten a very small amount of that large bowl of very delicious bisque, Jack and I ate the rest. It was the best that I have ever had and I'm still talking about it 50 years later.

We had a wonderful time with them. They took us to Mystic Sea Port and to a beautiful beach for swimming. We saw many other sights and I enjoyed talking with Jack about his work. He was a technical writer for submarine operational manuals. He had also been an officer in the Coast Guard.

Our week passed very quickly and as we drove home I told Marilyn about the decision I had made. As always she was very supportive of what I wanted to do.

When I returned to work on Monday I experienced something that you may read about but never expect to experience. Our statistical analyst was not at work when I arrived, and I had never known him to miss a day of work. Our manager was in a meeting and he had not said anything about Gene. I received a phone call from a local Jeweler later that morning asking me if he could speak to Gene. I told him that he had not come to work which was highly unusual because I had never known him to miss work. I have not seen him since that time.

Needless to say it disrupted our work and it took several months before another Gene that I recommended to our manager was transferred to our department and things began to get back to normal.

In late January I started to read several papers looking for sales opportunities. Keep in mind that we had no internet and I did not want my manager to know of my decision.

It was several weeks before I saw an advertisement that interested me. It was for a sales position with a company which I was not familiar with. It was a company that produced register books and stationery products for the funeral industry. Although I was hesitant about calling on funeral homes there would never be a major down turn in business.

I called for an interview and the sales manager, John, conducted the interview. He asked me many questions and then told me how impressed he was with the candidates that he had interviewed. He told me that he had several more people to interview and that he would call me for a second interview if I was chosen for the job.

I placed the whole matter in the Lord's hands. A couple of days later I was called for a second interview and accepted the offer that was made.

With very mixed emotions, I wrote my letter of resignation, stating that I would be leaving Ohio Brass

Company effective March 15, 1973. I had enjoyed a few days and eleven years with the company.

I also wrote a letter to my former manager, Al, who was now a district manager in Florida informing him of my decision. Within days, I received his letter of congratulations and more encouragement for my new endeavor.

Sales Time

But they that wait on the Lord shall renew their strength: They shall mount up with wings of eagles: They shall run and not walk: And they shall walk and not be faint.
Isaiah 40:31

I left Lexington on that mid March Sunday afternoon just after a severe ice storm. There were ice ruts 4 inches or more deep on the highway as I traveled west and there were times when I thought the car would get stuck on top of the ice. After several hours of driving I finally reached Auburn, Indiana and was relieved to check in at the motel.

Several of us began sales training on Monday morning. It was good training and after a few days, our training was complete. I returned home ready to make my first sales call. My manager, John, told me that he would like me to meet him in Toledo the following week to make a few calls with me and introduce me to a few people. I was pleased that he wanted to do so.

My territory consisted of twenty counties with Toledo being my largest city. I immediately developed a sales call schedule making sure that I would call on my major accounts quite frequently.

After becoming very familiar with our basic product line, I began to present product from our advertising specialty group of products. My sales were continuing to increase and I was getting to know some of the funeral directors quite well. It was a fun job.

There is nothing like making a large sale with a good commission. I never really experienced call reluctance as some new sales representatives are prone to experience.

I had worked for several months and was informed that a national funeral director's convention would be held in Cincinnati. I was expected to work our booth during the exhibit hours. It was a very large convention and I met many people.

I had brought Marilyn with me and we were invited to go with several others to dinner at the Beverly Hills restaurant. The person who had made the arrangements knew many of the people who worked at the establishment and we were escorted to see many of the rooms including the very large kitchen. I was shocked when that restaurant burned down several years after we were there.

During the convention we kept hearing someone from one of the music companies singing over the loud speakers. He had a beautiful voice and it almost commanded your full attention as he sang. My wife went to find where he was located. She came back to the booth and took me to meet him. It was Merrill Womack from Spokane, Washington.

He had survived a fiery plane crash, and though he had been badly burned and was terribly scarred, when he sang you never noticed it. What a voice!

I had been in my job for over a year and was very happy that I had made the move to sales work. A large funeral home in Toledo was redoing their office and I asked if they were selling their very large desk. The funeral director told me that he would sell both the desk and chair if I wanted them. I purchased both pieces and rented a large trailer to move them to Lexington. When I arrived Terry helped me move them to our basement. I used them for nearly sixteen years.

I was sitting at that desk when the phone rang. It was Carl. It had been nearly two years since I had seen him on our way to Connecticut. He told me he was looking for a sales rep to cover all of Michigan and all of Ohio and that he wanted me. I asked him why he wanted me and he told me that he did not know of anyone that would have done what I did. I asked him: "What do you mean? " He said that I had left a very good job to take a straight commission sales job with a wife, and three children under ten years old at home. I told him that I had Marilyn's blessing before doing so and that I was ready for a sales job.

He began to elaborate about the benefits of joining the company he was with. He mentioned that a company car was furnished and that all expenses were fully paid by the company. Gasoline prices at that time were making the major move from 25 cents per gallon to 50 cents per gallon and I was putting a lot of miles on my personal car. He also mentioned the vacation time such as two weeks at Christmas and the summer when schools were not in session.

All was falling on deaf ears because I had made the move to sales work and enjoyed my job very much. I was not interested in making a job change again. Carl was very persistent and told me to think about it, and that he would be calling in another week.

I gave no thought about it and was ready to tell him again that I really was not interested in the position. He called exactly when he said he would and reiterated what he had said in our previous conversation. I told him: "Carl, I am very sorry but I am really not interested in that position." He was very persistent and told me that he would be calling me again the following week.

I hung up the phone and I thought I had been hit with a brick. The Lord impressed on my heart: "You have not even prayed about this." I prayed to him: "Yes, Lord, you are right, I have not prayed about this matter and I am willing to change Jobs again, but please make it very clear if that is what you want me to do."

Carl called for the third time and I told him that I would consent to an interview. I also told him that we planned to leave for Michigan a week from Saturday and I would like to have the interview prior to leaving on vacation. He hung up the phone and called back five or ten minutes later and told me that the interview would be held at his home with his manager on the following Friday morning.

Carl also asked if we could pick up his son, Mickey, who had been visiting with our neighbors' two boys who lived several houses away from our home. He told me that his son would not be happy about it as he wanted to fly home. I told Carl that we would pick up his son about 9:00am on Thursday morning. Carl said that he would be calling him to let him know the arrangements that were made.

On Thursday morning we went to pick up Mickey and he was not happy. I was thankful that Carl had warned me of the situation.

For most of the eight hour drive to Carl's home we listened to Mickey expound about how we would not like Carl's manager, Herb. He told us that he was loud mouthed, foul mouthed, and a very arrogant man. I was not concerned about it because Carl had worked with or for him for over four years.

In addition, my football coach had prepared me well for whatever I might face in life with the training that we had endured.

We arrived that evening at Carl and Shirley's home in time for the evening meal. We were very happy to see them again and Carl and I ended up talking until long after the rest of the families had gone to bed. It must have been 1:30am or 2:00am when I climbed into bed. I knew from what Mickey had told us on the way to his home that Herb would be arriving about 7:00am even though he had a three hour drive to get to Carl's house.

I was up and dressed in a suit by 6:00am. I really had no questions about the job because Carl had told me all about his job when he was in Ohio. I was sitting in a chair having coffee and reading the paper, when, a little after7:00am, I heard a very loud knock on the door. No one else was up and it had been very quiet until Herb arrived.

I opened the door and said: "You must be Herb." He replied: "You must be Larry." We went outside on Carl's deck to talk to avoid waking anyone.

There is only so much you are able to discuss about a job and after getting to know each other, Herb stood up and asked if I wanted the job. Even though I was still somewhat reluctant about changing jobs again, I stood up and said: "Yes I do."

Herb immediately went to the phone and called his secretary, Sylvia. I heard him tell her to put me on the payroll immediately, and I waved my hand to tell him that I was leaving for vacation.

He hung up the phone and told me to go on vacation and have a good time. He said there would be an expense check waiting for me when I returned. He said Carl would be in contact with me and said: "Welcome aboard" and he left.

Carl and my wife may have been up before he left but I am not sure because it all happened so quickly. We enjoyed our time with Carl and Shirley and after having breakfast we left for Ohio.

All the way home I thought to myself: "What have I done?" It is one thing to leave a job when you are ready for a change. It is quite another to leave one when you are very happy with your position.

Marilyn and I arrived home and there was a letter from John, my manager with Messenger Company, telling me how pleased he was with my work and that he expected that my sales would continue to grow.

I became very nauseous thinking about what I would have to tell him on Monday.

Our neighbors, Toni and Terry were going with us on our trip to Michigan and I was glad for that. We packed our cars on Saturday morning and arrived at that very special place that evening.

We discussed my decision that evening and after eating, nausea struck again. Not pretty.

I made that call on Monday morning and John was stunned. He accepted it well and wished me the best.

We concluded our vacation and have wonderful memories from that trip with our neighbors.

Carl and Herb

I beseech you therefore brethren by the mercies of God, that ye present your bodies a living sacrifice, holy, acceptable unto God, which is your reasonable service.

And be not conformed to this world: but be ye transformed by the renewing of your mind that ye may prove what is that good, and acceptable, and perfect will of God.
Romans 12:1&2

After completing my work with Messenger Company, Carl called me to make arrangements to pick up my company car in Philadelphia. When I arrived he drove me to where the car was located. Of course, I had no idea where we were, but when we found the car, it was parked with garbage piled high next to the curb. It was a four door Ford LTD and was locked.

Carl went somewhere to obtain a key while I stayed with the car. He obtained the key and when I opened the door, I was shocked. There were cigarette butts over 4 inches high on the front passenger side of the car. The back of the car had sacks of leftover meals piled to the roof of the car. It smelled worst than a garbage truck.

After cleaning out the trash, Carl gave me a handful of sales catalogs and told me that he planned to come to Ohio the following week to make sales calls with me.

The first thing I did after arriving home was to take the car to a car wash and have it cleaned inside and out.

Carl was not coming until Tuesday, so I decided to make a few calls on Monday with catalogs. I did not have product to show, however I would be able to get some information. The catalog was two pages only and was tri folded. Our product consisted of a junior high health text, a senior high health text, and science workbook/lab manuals that were correlated to the major science texts from other publishers. There were also materials for the regent exams for New York.

The purpose of my sales calls was to find out if health was taught as a separate course in the junior high school and, if so, how old, was their textbook. If the teacher was using a text over five years old I would sample a copy of our book along with a price list. Naturally I would point out some special features when I had a text to present.

High schools in Ohio generally had certified health teachers in the physical education department who taught the course to ninth grade students.

I would also make contact with the various science teachers to find out which textbooks they were using and to ask if they used lab manuals for their courses. I would try to show our materials whether they were using labs or not.

On my first sales calls I could not present product, but, I could obtain information for follow up, if necessary. The name of our company was CEBCO [College Entrance Book Company} which was owned by Standard Publishing. When I introduced myself, I would give my name and that I was with CEBCO Publishing Co. I received many replies: "CEBCO who?" It was an interesting experience.

Carl came to pick me up and we made sales calls in the Canton area where he had spent considerable time when he lived in Ohio. We had product and Carl taught me how to present it. He also gave me information concerning joining the Ohio Professional Bookmen's Association.

It was an organization of educational sales representatives that published a booklet that contained the names of many publishing companies, along with the names of sales representatives, and their territories.

The organization also hosted exhibits at various locations where teachers and administrators could preview materials and request samples.

I was excited to attend my first exhibit and to display our materials. I was not only looking forward to meeting teachers and curriculum directors, but also was interested in meeting my fellow sales representatives. I had much to learn about educational sales and they could help me understand the industry.

OPBA was a fraternity of sales representatives and I was formally inducted into the organization. We all agreed to abide by the professional guidelines that had been established and published. That induction ceremony was discontinued shortly after I was inducted and I was blessed to have begun my educational career during a very special time in the publishing industry.

I developed a grading system for myself as a result of my marketing experience. I kept track of every junior high school, high school, and how many teachers I had contact with on a daily basis.

I also developed a sales call schedule to work eighty per cent of my Ohio territory before calling on schools in Michigan.

The one thing that I had a hard time getting used to was, I never knew if I was making any sales. I had been used to being able to totaling my sales for each day and knowing how much I was making for that day. Carl kept assuring me to just keep doing what I was doing and that the orders would start to come in during April and increase each month through the summer.

I made my first trip to Michigan in late February or early March and obtained information about the Michigan Educational Sales Representatives Association. Most of their exhibits had been held in the fall. I made several weeks of sales calls during the spring and made arrangements to join their sales organization.

I had completed most of the work that I had planned for Michigan when Carl called and asked me to meet him in Buffalo. He also told me to bring some fishing equipment as he planned to take me trout fishing one evening after work.

When I arrived at the hotel the following week Carl introduced me to a Prentice Hall sales representative whose name was Tim. The three of us talked for fifteen or twenty minutes and Carl asked me if I liked liver and onions. I told him that I did and the two of us went to dinner.

As he was driving us to the restaurant, he told me that liver and onions was the special for the evening and that the restaurant would be packed. He went on to say that the restaurant was not much to look at from the outside but the inside was very nice and would be full of professional people.

He went on to explain that when we entered the building, we would be met by the head waiter and he would give us a time when we could be expected to be seated. He said that he was very good at seating people at the time designated.

We entered the restaurant and were met by the waiter and he gave us a time when he expected to seat us. The restaurant was full of professionally dressed people as Carl said it would be. There was a long straight bar on the left and there was a line of fairly small tables going down the center of the restaurant. There were larger tables along the right side.

There were two bar stools available and Carl and I sat down. Carl ordered his drink and I had my usual diet coke. At the appointed time we were escorted to one of the center tables, which was about eight inches from the table beside ours. A waiter appeared instantly and we ordered our meals and soon became involved discussing our work plans for the next day.

Sometime during our discussion two ladies were seated at the table next to ours. We did not acknowledge them as we were involved in our conversation and the two of them were also involved in a discussion. A short time after they were seated the lady sitting next to me dropped her napkin and I picked it up for her and we became involved in a short conversation with them. She happened to be from Lexington where Carl had lived while in Ohio and where I currently was living. She was connected with one of the music stores in Mansfield.

Our meals arrived and Carl was absolutely right. Out of the thousands of meals that I have eaten at restaurants, I have discussed that meal of liver and onions more than any other meal that I have eaten with the possible exception of the lobster bisque which Marilyn's cousin made for us.

Carl and I went directly to the hotel after we had eaten and sat down with maps to mark where the schools that we planned to call on were located. He also went over the order book and the brief review books. We agreed to meet back at the hotel to determine where we would eat our evening meal.

When I arrived at that first school the next day it was unlike any sales call I have ever made. The secretary was very accommodating and was used to sales representatives coming to the school and basically taking orders for brief review books in the spring of the year. Brief review books were used by students to help them prepare for the regents exams. She directed me to the regent course teachers and when they saw me at their door at an appropriate time they would tell me how many books they wanted to order. Not all calls went as smoothly as that first call but many of them did. I enjoyed the experience.

I arrived back at the hotel at the end of the day and went over my work with Carl. He asked me what I would like to do for dinner and I told him that I had eaten at the Niagara Falls Club on the Canadian side of the falls when I was working for Ohio Brass. I had seen the revolving restaurant on top of a sphere and would enjoy going there for dinner. He agreed and had me drive.

When we arrived at customs, the custom officer saw the cartons I had in back and told me that I would have to unload them and leave them with him. I pointed to the restaurant and told him that the cartons contained school books and that, if he wanted American dollars to be spent in Canada, he would allow us to go to the restaurant and eat. Otherwise, I would find another restaurant in Buffalo. He told us to go ahead.

We enjoyed the meal very much and I particularly enjoyed the view of the falls from our position. On the way back to the hotel Carl told me to plan on meeting him at a location on the Cattaraugus River near Hamburg after work the next day. We would do some trout fishing.

We arrived at the river about the same time. Carl was dressed immaculately, as usual. He looked like he was a model for Orvis. He had on wading boots, matching pants and vest, along with state of the art fishing equipment. He was very gracious as he opened his tackle box when he told me I could use whatever lure I would like to use. I told him thanks but I would try what I had first.

He walked into the very clear and swift moving current of the river. I stood on shore dressed in a pair of Levis and light jacket. I was also wearing my Air Force brogans that had been issued to me in 1962. We had fished for nearly an hour and neither of us had caught a fish.

I glanced across the river and Carl was standing objectively near a submerged log dipping a lure into the stream. He lifted his line to change lures and I called across to him and asked him to put the lure on my line when I cast over to him.

He did and I retrieved the lure to where I was standing and cast it into the rapids about twenty yards upstream from where Carl was standing. I immediately thought I was snagged behind a rock until I felt a significant tug on my line. I ended up catching a very nice trout on my first cast with the lure that Carl had been using for quite a long time. I made several more casts to the same location and caught three or four smaller trout within five minutes. There is nothing like beginners' luck.

Sometime during the four days I spent with Carl he took me to meet Joe, the author of our high school Health text. I was very pleased to meet him.

I called on schools the next day and headed back to Ohio. I was glad to have spent some more time with Carl. I finished my first selling season calling on schools in Ohio. Herb did not require an annual report and we did not have a summer meeting. I began enjoying the summer vacation.

OPBA did have a summer meeting which I attended. After a short business meeting I played golf with some of the other sales reps. It was a good meeting and I was glad to get to know some of my fellow sales reps.

I began coaching little league softball and after a couple of years coaching, I became an umpire. What an experience that was. I also began playing tennis with my neighbor Terry. He beat me badly for several years until I became more competitive.

During the fall of 1975 I concentrated on trying to increase sales in Michigan. I enjoyed working the exhibits and met many teachers along with meeting fellow sales reps working in Michigan. One of them was a Prentice Hall sales rep named Cal. We had much in common and became good friends. After working the exhibits during the day we enjoyed many evening meals together.

I quickly observed two major differences between Michigan schools and Ohio schools. Michigan schools were able to purchase educational materials more frequently than Ohio schools. It was also interesting to note that the senior high health course was taught in several different areas in Michigan schools. Some schools taught the course in the home economics department, some schools had social studies teachers teaching it, and in some schools there was a health department separate from the physical education department.

One morning I was working in either Grand Rapids or Lansing and I rushed out of the hotel to go to a nearby school. The secretary was very accommodating and she took me to see a science teacher. Before school began I had seen everyone that I had wanted to see and I went to a Bob Evans restaurant to eat breakfast. I was sitting at the table reading the morning paper and I noticed sever people looking at me rather strangely. I had no idea why until I picked up my fork and saw that I had put on pin stripped pants from one suit and was wearing the suit coat from another pin stripped suit. No one that I had talked to in the school mentioned it because they probably never noticed. I finished breakfast and returned to my room to put on the matching jacket.

Herb rarely worked with me and when he did it was usually at a convention. We were up several hours before the convention opened for the day and we spent some time getting to know each other. He told me that he majored in chemical engineering but had spent most of his career in publishing. I fully understood because the ink had replaced my blood, also.

I noticed that he would read the telephone book. I began to do the same and I learned much local history of the communities where I stayed. I also, always read the local newspaper in addition to reading USA Today or the Wall Street Journal. Many times I would be talking with a teacher who had lived in the area and told them something about their community that they did not know.

Herb did however have a habit that greatly disturbed me. We would be enjoying a dinner together and for whatever reason, if the waitress was not pleasing him, he would voice his displeasure in a very loud voice. I made sure to note the restaurants that he was pleased with to avoid this habit of his whenever it was possible to do so.

I was working an exhibit in Michigan when a teacher asked me if I had taught school before beginning my sales career. I told him about my three hour teaching experience when I was in high school. I was sitting in a study hall when the superintendent walked up to me and asked if I would please go to the elementary school and teach a class of second or third graders for a few hours. Apparently a teacher became ill and had to leave. I met the class and we reviewed times tables for awhile and then we picked out a book and I had each student read a paragraph and pass it on to the next student. We did this for quite some time. I don't remember what else I had them do, but the time passed quickly for me. That was the total teaching experience that I had prior to entering my educational sales career.

I also told him about my brief sales experience with Messenger Company, and he told me that my former manager along with many of the sales people, were no longer employed with Messenger. There had been a complete reorganization of the company. Had I not changed jobs I would have lost my sales job along with the rest of them. Thank You Lord.

I was working in the Ann Arbor area one winter and I saw many people cross country skiing on the golf course located near one of the high schools. I thought that would be a good thing for me to do.

Several weeks later I was talking to a supervisor from one of the districts and told him about what I had seen. He was also a skier and told me that a nearby rental place was selling some of their used equipment. I ended up purchasing all of my equipment for nineteen dollars and thirty-one cents. I began skiing a few times while in Michigan but spent many Sunday afternoons on a golf course in Ohio. It was great exercise, and I used that equipment for over 30 years.

Before I left for my sales trips to Michigan, I would be sure to have at least 30 health texts and a quantity of workbook lab manuals to take with me. Those workbook lab manuals were an updated version of the ones I had used in high school and I was now in the job that I had thought, while there, would be a good job to have.

I would sit down with a map and carefully plan my sales calls, before starting my day. I wasted no time looking for buildings. Initially every call was a cold call, and I had no appointments. My first question would be when seeing a health teacher was: "How old is your textbook?" If it was four years or older, I would point out several features of our book and ask if they had any questions. I would open the price list, and circle the text with the price and hand both the text and price list to them. I would thank them for their time and move on to the science teachers and approach them the same way except I would ask what text they were using. I would also ask if they used lab manuals. I then would point out the cross reference in our workbook to their text, and hand it to them along with the price list.

I was told several times that I was very direct in stating my business and they liked that, as I was not wasting their time. I had not thought about it, as my objective was to make contact with as many teachers in a day that I could. Believe it or not, I had one day when I was in thirteen buildings and had seen over 100 teachers. It was an exceptional day where the buildings were close to each other and many teachers were available when I called on them.

Herb required daily call reports and I knew that he read them from the discussions that we had. I was a few days behind in mailing them to him when I received an early morning phone call from him. He told me that he wanted to meet me in Youngstown for lunch the following week. He also told me to bring Marilyn with me. I had no idea what he wanted. His wife was travelling with him to Minneapolis for their state health convention.

Marilyn and I arrived at the designated restaurant I had chosen at the same time as Herb and his wife pulled into the parking lot. He introduced his wife to us and I introduced Marilyn to them. He wasted no time in telling us why he wanted to see us.

He said before we order lunch I will tell you why I wanted to meet with you. I would like you to move to California to be our west coast sales manager. He had explored Mission Viejo and knew that there were Christian schools in the area because he knew that we had our children enrolled in a Christian elementary school. He told us that when the school year ended we could drive to California and take our time looking for a home. We ate lunch and before leaving he said: "Think it over and give me your decision next week."

On our drive home, Marilyn told me that whatever decision I made she would support.

Every book that I have ever read suggested that before making a major change in your life it would be advisable to discuss that change with a few knowledgeable people that you trust before making a decision. I followed that advice and I called Joe, the sales engineer who had been to Los Angeles more times than any one I knew.

We met for lunch and after discussing the situation with him the first question he asked was: "Do any of your children have allergies?" I had not thought of this. Every time that Joe would return from L A. his eyes would water for several days because of the terrible fog in that city, at that time. All three of our children had some form of allergy.

I next called a realtor in Mission Viejo and he informed me that homes were selling within hours of being listed and prices were escalating every day. Mission Viejo was mission impossible for us.

I called Herb and thanked him for the opportunity, but I felt that we should remain in Ohio. He was very understanding, and I continued working in Michigan and Ohio.

I had not attended college for 3 years and I still needed some hours to complete my degree. I made arrangements to attend the University of Akron and transfer the credits to Ashland. When I finished and the credits were transferred I still needed one credit hour.

My sales had increased each year and I was bothered that there was not a commission plan. I discussed it with Herb and he told me that he was not able to have one.

I had met another sales representative in my first or second year in the business and he told me that he was moving to California with his company later in the year. There was a commission plan with his company, and it involved calling on both, public and school librarians. It sounded interesting, and he told me to think about it, and let him know if I would like to have his job when he moved. He assured me that when the time came for him to move that he could get me the job.

The time came for Larry to move to California and I told him that I would like to be considered for his job. I was interviewed and offered the job. I accepted it, and called Herb in November to let him know what I planned to do and why. He was very nice about it.

I flew to Madison, Wisconsin for what turned out to be a ten day video recorded sales training program. There were several other sales trainees, and I was glad to not be the only one.

Demco had purchased a small publishing company that published library books. In addition to learning about the furniture line and book repair business, we also were introduced to the book jobbing business. It was an interesting experience. We had eaten at some of the best restaurants in Madison all week, and I was happy to stay in the hotel and have a hamburger for dinner. Their hot cider was very good also.

I returned home a few days before Christmas and was told by Bill, our regional sales manager, to plan on flying to Boston, in January, for another meeting. I don't remember much about the meeting, but I do remember an interesting meal.

It had snowed over twenty inches in one day and college girls were cross country skiing to the hotel to eat. We were staying at the Ritz Carlton on the commons. The college girls had no problem being seated while wearing their ski attire but when we went down stairs to the restaurant, we were told that we must wear jackets and ties before we could be seated.

Bill was from Boston, and when we met at the elevator wearing our ties, Bill had his jacket buttons going down his back with the tie on backwards. We arrived to be seated, and the waiter seated us, saying nothing.

I returned home and I had a book repair workshop scheduled in Marietta. It was snowing very hard, and when I walked to the car to leave, Marilyn rushed out of the house and told me that someone had called to tell me that the workshop had been cancelled because of the snow.

I was glad that she had called because it was the beginning of the blizzard of "78" which completely covered a truck in snow for a week. The driver, Jim Truly, was snowed in his truck cab for most of that time before he was rescued.

When the snow cleared and the schools reopened, I was able to begin work in my new job. The territory also included western Pennsylvania. I made a trip to Pittsburg and met many librarians. I spent more time with them than I did with teachers, because of the product that I was now selling.

Things were going well when something occurred that helped me to face a totally unexpected turn of events.

A very well known pastor, Knute Larson, who was the pastor of a large church in Akron, was scheduled to speak at our church. I had met Pastor Larson years earlier when he was dating his wife while attending seminary.

I have heard several thousand messages in my life and most of them were very good but his message is the only one that I remember. It was given on April 28, 1978 and the title was: "Jesus Christ is Worth Following."

I am not going to get into the details of the message, but his three points were:

DECIDE – We must all make a decision.
DEDICATE – If we decide that Jesus is worth following, dedicate every area of your life to him and him alone.

DEVELOP – Lasting patterns in Jesus Christ one day at a time.

That message spoke to me more than any message that I have heard. I had been a Christian for many years, but had not read the scripture completely through.

I began reading the Scofield Reference Bible that my wife had given to me prior to our marriage. I did not try to read it in a year. I read it along with all of Scofield's notes over a period of a year and a half.

I had been and am in the habit of reading "Our Daily Bread" each morning. But, if we are serious about our belief it is critical to read his word.

In June, I received a call from Bill advising me that Larry had decided to return to Ohio. He wanted me to meet him in Youngstown, to divide the territory, to take effect when Larry returned. I met him, and we spent considerable time doing that on a Friday afternoon. All the while, I told Bill we were wasting our time, because it was one territory when Larry left, and I seriously doubted that it would become two. I told him that I would be let go when he returned.

The phone rang on Monday morning, and when I answered, it was Bill. There was silence for a moment and I said: "Bill, just tell me, it is not your fault that Larry decided to return." He was very remorse and told me that I would receive six weeks of severance compensation.

Another pastor friend of mine, who was selling insurance on a part time basis, told me that I now had no excuse for not getting my insurance license. I studied and did get my license. I worked with Frank, and we had fun selling together, but it just was not what I wanted to do.

I finally called the sales rep, who, had picked up the company car when I left CEBCO, to ask if Herb had replaced me. He told me that he had not, and called him to let him know I would like to return. Herb called me and welcomed me back. He told me that, because of what I had done, he was able to get a commission plan approved. The Lord is good.

I was back in the job that I really liked and was running hard. I had kept all of my call records and now was seeing many teachers for the second or third time since I began working for the company.

Herb and his wife normally took a lengthy cruise in the spring and he had called to let me know that they would be gone for two or three weeks. I updated my records when I made calls but became lazy about sending them to Herb since he was gone. I miscalculated when he would return.

The phone rang on an early Monday morning and it was Herb. The first words I heard were: "Larry I expect your reports. I write them myself and I expect yours. Understood?" I replied: "Yes sir." I told him how things were going and we hung up.

I felt very bad about what I had done. I was ashamed of myself because there was no logical reason for it except plain laziness. It was a very poor Christian testimony.

Our Daily Bread devotional reading that morning was based on Romans 12:1-2 shown at the head of this chapter. As I read those verses over and over, I was determined to memorize them and do my best to apply them for the rest of my life.

Doing that one thing has stopped me from doing many things that I might have done and has spurred me on to do as many or more things that I really did not feel like doing.

CEBCO had continued to publish additional product, and we now had a middle school science program along with a Chemistry textbook to sell.

Herb called and wanted me to work in Detroit with me for a day. It was late May and schools were getting ready to conclude the year. I decided to follow up with a few teachers from whom I was expecting to receive orders.

This was the first and only time that Herb made building calls with me. It turned out to be a very unpleasant experience. We had made several calls and all was going well until I was driving to a school which I had not been to in several months. I made a left turn and quickly realized that I should have made a right turn. I turned around and Herb exploded. He accused me of not knowing my territory and went on ranting and raving until I pulled into the school parking lot. By that time, I was also angry, and ready to throw him out of the car.

I returned to Ohio with a determination to totally unload on him when the occasion presented itself. It bothered me all summer. He called and wanted me to pick him up at the airport in Columbus to go to a convention in Kentucky in late August or early September. We treated each other cordial enough but I was still determined that I was not going to take anymore of his yelling at me.

I picked him up at the airport and as we were driving to Kentucky, it became very obvious that he had come with a determination to treat me with respect no matter what happened. We really did have great respect for each other. Although he was loud, he was very careful to not use foul language when talking with me.

As we continued our trip, he asked me a question that I never would have expected from him. He asked me if our church provided for our pastor with good financial support. I told him that we tried to do so. He then went on to tell me that their rabbi was provided for very well.

We continued driving in silence for a while and all of a sudden he exploded with: "I hate Christians." I calmly asked him "Why?" He responded by telling me that they think that they are always right. I knew that he was referring to their belief and I responded by asking him if he had ever considered the possibility that they were indeed right? He exploded again and told me that he thought he was becoming an atheist. I told him: "Herb, you know that is not true." There was no point in continuing the discussion because he knew of my firm belief that Jesus is their Messiah.

Herb and I did not work together again until several months later. The state Science Convention was being held in Cincinnati during February and he came to help me with it. He told me that the president of CEBCO would be attending and that we would be going to dinner with him.

Perdue joined us at the exhibit booth and when we were through working for the day we went to a restaurant that he had selected. It was located at the top of a fairly tall building overlooking the Ohio River. It was a beautiful, clear evening, and the view was wonderful.

The restaurant was very busy and the food was delicious. When we finished eating, the waitress came to ask if we were having dessert. I had eaten so much that I declined but Herb had seen those tall glasses of strawberries, covered with whipped cream, and he could not resist indulging. Perdue also declined having any.

As the waitress was approaching our table with Herb's very tall glass of strawberries, covered with an ample amount of whipped cream, she tripped over something and Herb was instantly bathed with strawberries, ice cream, and whipped cream. I burst out laughing, because if anyone deserved it, he did. I said: "Herb that dessert looks so good on you I think I will have some. The three of us ended up eating dessert.

CEBCO had published a biology text and we had a meeting in New Jersey to meet the author and learn about the text. It was a beautiful text, and I was anxious to begin presenting it to teachers.

When schools opened in the fall, I began running hard with that new book. We were beginning to win quite a number of adoptions with both our chemistry and now biology texts. This did not go unnoticed by the major publishers.

Cal and I were having dinner at the Holiday Inn in Saginaw one evening, after we had worked an exhibit. It was probably late April or early May and, as we were talking, he asked me what I thought about him becoming a manager. He had worked quite a number of years as a sales rep for Prentice Hall Publishing Company and I asked him if that was what he wanted to do? He told me that he thought he was ready to become a manager. I told him to go for it, and that if it didn't work out, he could always return to being a sales rep. I knew that he was diligently making his sales calls, because I had met many teachers who knew him.

Cal had told me that Prentice Hall was publishing a biology textbook and the author was a very well known science supervisor from Michigan who I knew quite well. I was looking forward to see what the text looked like.

One of my last sales calls that year, was at a school district twenty or thirty miles north of where Cal lived. It was late in the school year, and the end of the day, when I arrived and requested to see the biology teachers. They were planning to purchase new texts for the following year and agreed to see me before leaving for the day. Cal had been there with his new text and they were planning to pur-chase it. I asked to see it and I was shocked to see such small illustrations.

I spent about ten minutes with those teachers comparing the CEBCO text with the Prentice Hall text and by the time I left they had decided to purchase ours.

When I began working the exhibits in Michigan that fall, I did not see Cal and I presumed that he had become a manager.

There was a large meeting scheduled for mid October in Marquette. I had not made a sales trip to the upper peninsula of Michigan, because I had not had enough material to justify doing so. CEBCO now had a large enough product line that I thought it would be worth doing.

I left home on a Sunday afternoon and drove to Mount Pleasant. On Monday morning I began working my way north calling on as many schools that I could. I scheduled my time to allow me to call on Newberry and Munising schools, before they were closed for the day on Thursday.

I left Munising about 3:30 in the afternoon to drive to Marquette to set up my display before dinner. There was no traffic on the highway and even though the speed limit was fifty-five miles per hour, I soon was going over seventy and watching very closely for any animal that might run in front of me. I also glanced in the mirror frequently.

As I was driving on a long straight stretch of highway a Michigan trooper passed me going eighty miles per hour or more and, turned and waved goodbye to me. His was one of maybe three cars that I saw on the highway that evening before arriving in Marquette.

The exhibit was very well attended, and I was pleased that I had made the trip. I met many teachers and gave samples of our material to them for examination.

While working the state Science Convention in Lansing, I met teachers and students from the UP that had told me of a beautiful golf course near Copper Harbor. I had my golf clubs with me, since I planned to stay in Marquette for the weekend.

I left to drive to the course early Saturday morning and, when I arrived about noon, there was four inches of snow everywhere. I did manage to find a small restaurant that was open, and I had lunch. I enjoyed talking to the owner and learned many things about the area.

On Monday morning, I began calling on the larger school districts of the western UP. I enjoyed doing so as not only were the teachers and administrators happy to see a new face, but the scenery was beautiful.

I was speaking to a chemistry teacher from one the districts at the end of the day, and he told me about life in the UP. We had an interesting discussion, and I presented our chemistry program to him. I had used some terminology that I had learned from the hundreds of teachers that I had seen, and he asked me how long I had taught chemistry. I told him that all I know about chemistry could be written on a pinhead. I went on to tell him that all the terminology I knew, came from asking many questions and many teachers, like him, had been kind enough to educate me a little.

I told him that I had majored in business, and whenever I was talking to a teacher, and they used a term that I was unfamiliar with, I would tell them that I was a dumb business major and to please explain what the term meant. They were always very gracious and would explain what they were speaking about.

How are you in your Christian life? Do you know the terminology as I did, but have not explored much more. I attended church one time and the minister held up his Bible and commented on what a gold mine it was. I did not have any idea of what he was talking about at the time, but, Thank You Lord I have done much mining since.

As I was crossing the bridge to return to the Lower Peninsula, on the Thursday evening of the last week in October that year, I saw one of the most beautiful sights that I have ever seen. The sun was setting in Lake Michigan, and when I looked east, there was a beautiful bright full moon rising out of Lake Huron. I turned off my lights, while crossing the bridge, to see ice particles shining in the moonlight on the road. There was not a cloud in the sky.

I returned home and completed the school year. I had enjoyed the summer and was working in Ohio when I received a call from Herb.

He told me that CEBCO had been acquired by Allyn and Bacon Publishing Company and that he would be retiring. He suggested that I might want to get a job with one of our competitors and to keep working until I heard something. I thanked him for his call and wished him well.

I hung up the phone not sure what I should do. I had gained much experience with CEBCO and had worked in several states. I had learned how to obtain information from various sources, had met thousands of educators, and become friends with many sales reps.

I continued working and was working at one of the exhibits when a very experienced sales representative came up to me and said: "Larry I know what you are going through. I have been through it several times. Just ride the train for as long as you can." I thanked George for his kind words and advice.

The Mergers

Let not your heart be troubled: ye believe in God, believe also in me.

John 14:1

Merger 1

I received a call from Jack, the manager of Ohio for Allyn and Bacon Publishing Company, and he asked me to come to Boston for an interview.

When I arrived at the office, the first words I heard upon entering the building were: "Fire him." The national sales manager had spoken them to someone. I met with Jack and had a good interview with him and was retained as a sales representative for part of Ohio. Thank you Lord!

He told me that he would be coming to Ohio to meet with the other two sales reps and would like me to join them in Cincinnati. I had met one of the sales reps, Ted, but did not know Bonnie, who had been recently hired. We met at the hotel and we three reps spent considerable time dividing the state into three territories, which Jack approved.

I went over the CEBCO product with Ted and Bonnie, and they went over Allyn and Bacon product with me. We worked our territories and flew to Washington D.C. for the winter sales meeting in January. I met several other representatives from the region, and we practiced making presentations to each other. It was a good meeting, and I learned a lot about the product.

After I returned home, Jack called and wanted to work with me in Cleveland. We worked well together. I had him make some calls on Latin teachers while I saw science teachers.

I had seen in the news that Simon & Schuster had purchased Prentice Hall Publishing Company and was curious what was going to happen, since they had acquired Allyn and Bacon only a matter of months prior to the PH acquisition. Allyn and Bacon management was quite certain that they would be in control, if the two companies were merged.

We continued to work as separate companies through the school year, and I was acquiring considerable knowledge about the social studies product line. I enjoyed meeting social studies teachers, and they taught me a lot about their courses. Allyn and Bacon also had a mathematics program, which I was beginning to get a handle on.

While working one of the exhibits, I met the new Prentice Hall sales representative for the Cleveland area. I had known their previous rep for the territory, but had not met Paul. During the course of our conversation, I pointed out the differences between the CEBCO biology text and Prentice Hall's new text. Paul got very angry and told Ted I was arrogant.

This should be interesting, if and when the companies merged.

Sure enough, I received a call from Cal, late May, and he told me he was my manager. I had not talked to Cal since our dinner in Saginaw that had taken place two years previous to this call. When he told me that he was my manager I asked him if he was hiring me or firing me, since I knew that there were already two PH sales reps in Ohio. He told me that one rep was no longer with them; Ted, Paul, and I would be the sales representatives for Ohio. I also told him that we had been friends for many years and, if I was doing something that he did not approve of, not to let friendship prevent him from telling me.

Merger 2

He told me to meet with Ted and Paul, to estimate the total sales he could expect from Ohio, for the following year. I made arrangements with them to meet at our home, since it was more centrally located.

Ted and Paul arrived at our home, and we began to work immediately, going through all of the catalogs, estimating the sales total for the state, line item by line item. Paul was initially very cool to me, but as we continued to work, we jelled into a formative sales team. We spent over three hours working on that project, and gave Cal our number. Amazingly, when all sales were in for the year, we had underestimated by less than three per cent.

While we were at our house, we developed our own territories by school enrollment, and presented them to Cal. Cal presented it to management and our territories were approved as presented.

We were then given annual business plan assignments for each of our territories. We were to develop a four month calendar showing our planned sales calls for each day. We were to include a myriad of details, showing how we planned to achieve our sales goals, which, we would receive later. It was like writing a term paper.

When it was time to go to the annual sales meeting in Florida, I called Ted and we flew down together. Upon arrival, we checked in and were assigned roommates for the meeting. I met Mike, from Illinois, who was my roommate, and I liked him. He was the cleanest smoker that I have ever met. He did not smoke in the room, and I never knew he smoked, until I saw him smoking outside between one of the meetings.

There were nearly four hundred people in attendance and most of them were former teachers. After watching several days of presentations by many different sales and product developers, we were all together in a general session, and I thought that there was so much talent in the room, I was not even sure I belonged there. I prayed to the Lord: "With your help, I will give it my best, and trust you for the results." I was very thankful for the time I spent with both a small company and the limited time with Allyn and Bacon prior to this merger.

To learn product about every discipline, and most of the time, multiple programs for the same discipline was an overwhelming task. The presenters were very good, and by the end of that marathon training meeting I felt confident enough to begin presenting most of the material to teachers.

I returned home and began working my new territory. I now had a full product line and it was necessary to alter my sales call procedure. I first called on high schools and tried to see as many department heads as possible, and would make notes concerning their availability, by checking their planning periods. I would do the same for the middle schools or junior high schools. I would then try to make contact with the district curriculum director before continuing on to the next district. It was becoming more of relationship building in addition to presenting programs. My territory, of course, was smaller geographically, and I was better able to build those relationships necessary to increase sales.

Cal called and wanted to work with me. He may have driven from Grand Rapids or I may have picked him up at the Toledo airport, but the first thing he wanted to do was have a donut and coffee. I had known him but was completely unaware of his donut addiction. We had much fun over the years about this.

We had a great time working together, and because of his vast knowledge about the Prentice Hall programs, I was able to learn many tips from him about presenting those programs.

Paul, Ted, and I would always work the state conventions together. We quickly developed into a solid sales team. Occasionally, we would host Prentice Hall functions after the exhibit hours were over. Paul and Ted would serve soft drinks and wine from the bar, and I would mingle with our guests. It worked very well.

Fred, our southern Florida sales representative, requested permission to have Ted and I fly to Florida to help him sell chemistry texts. We did and had a great week working with Fred and his manager, Wendell.

Meanwhile, Cal had called me to tell me that the president of Prentice Hall wanted to work with me. He had been working with sales reps because he was still in the process of reducing the sales force, since the merger had taken place.

I had talked to Kevin, the New Jersey sales rep, the previous summer, and he told me what to expect, since he had worked with him. I asked Cal to have him fly into Dayton, when I returned from Florida, and to let me know when he would be arriving.

It was late spring, and I planned on following up on several presentations that I had made involving significant sized orders. I also had received a large order for our middle school science program, and we were having difficulty getting software sent to them, as promised.

I had planned a very full day, and would have worked that way whether or not the president was with me. I picked him up at the airport and we walked into our first school ten minutes later. As we entered, the science department head that I wanted to see, was in the office. I introduced Jim to her and told him about the problem I was having getting software delivered to her.

He walked directly to the phone and could not get anyone to answer his call. We told her that I would be back to advise her when she could expect delivery. We saw a couple of other teachers, and went to the next school.

We continued going school to school with very little time between our sales calls. By that time I was fairly well known by the secretaries and teachers, but I have had very few days in my career when things went as well as they did that day. The teachers, who I wanted to see, were available when I wanted to see them. The Lord had to have planned that day.

We walked into the last high school of the day and as we entered the social studies department head was walking down the hall toward us. He said: "Hi, Larry, you will be interested to know that our department met last evening and we plan to purchase 500 government books from you." I introduced Jim and thanked him for the order. After a short conversation, we departed.

I had made an appointment with one of the supervisors from Dayton Public Schools for the last call of the day.

We were on our way to U.S. route 70 and Jim noticed a White Castle restaurant and asked if we could stop there. We had not stopped for lunch and he was very hungry. He walked to the counter and ordered five hamburgers. When I heard him order, I walked directly up to him and said: "Jim, you cannot have that many, we do not have time for you to eat them. You may have two." I did not care if he was the president, he was in my territory and he was working with me.

We made the appointment and had a good meeting with the supervisor. Our day ended about 4:30 or 5:00pm.

Jim was scheduled to work with Ted the next day, but called him to tell him he was ill, and would not be able to meet him. I think I took him back to the airport that evening, but am not sure.

I had very little, if any, contact with him for the rest of his time with Prentice Hall. He established his own company, and I saw him at one of the conventions in Indianapolis several years after he left PH. I brought up our experience that we had because I felt that he thought that I had pre arranged all that took place. That just would not have been possible with the schedule that I had. His response was: "Don't you just wish this could go on forever." Selling educational materials to educators was indeed fun!

Merger 3

It had been several years since the merger of Allyn and Bacon with Prentice Hall and many other publishing companies were going through the same thing. Scott Foresman was now being merged with Prentice Hall. We now had several biology textbooks and it was time to go see my friend, Dick, who had told me that he was not interested in anything I had to sell when I was with CEBCO.

I called the Principal to find out what time he would be available. When I arrived, Steve, the Principal, told me to go to his room to see him. I walked into his room and said: "Dick, here are several Biology texts to look over. I don't know anything about biology and you know it all." I put them on his lab table and told him to call me if he was interested in one of them. I then turned and walked out.

About four or five weeks later Dick called me and told me that he would like to purchase one of the texts. I asked for an appointment and went to see him. When I saw him I asked him to tell me why he wanted to purchase that particular text. He told me that he spent quite a bit of time teaching genetics and that the text had the best material about genetics that he had seen in a high school biology test. I thanked him for the order, and we have had several conversations since that time. He is a very good outdoor writer and I read his articles in our local paper.

I went to the Dayton area where one of the authors of the text that Dick had purchased was teaching. I saw Gary, and told him of my experience with Dick, and he responded: "I should be honored. I wrote that portion of the text."

Prentice Hall was in the process of forming sales advisory councils for the purpose of obtaining information from sales representatives to help with product development. I was requested to serve on one of them and I welcomed the opportunity. It gave me a chance to meet and spend some time with several colleagues who were in the marketing department. I also became aware of product that was being developed. There were several new sales reps, whom I had not met, on the council and I enjoyed meeting them.

The first day, which had been very intense and packed with a heavy agenda ended, and Chuck, from the office asked: "Are any of you interested in going to the race track for their buffet?" Several of us went and the food was delicious.

I am not much of a gambler, but I did place a wager on a couple of horses. When we returned to the hotel, a number of us were sitting on a bench lining the wall of the entrance way. Chuck walked in and asked how we did. If the person had lost money he gave them the amount they had lost. He did that for everyone. He had won a fair amount of money and was sharing his winnings.

It made me think: "Would I have done that?" I am not sure that I would have, but it sure made me aware of what I should be doing.

I was making sales calls in the Dayton area, one November day, and I met a new young science teacher. She had gone to college and worked hard to become a teacher, and after three months, she was so disappointed that she was ready to quit.

She was buried with teaching four or five different courses which required considerable preparation time and she did not have textbooks for her students. She was nearly crying as she told me of her situation.

After listening to her, I told her that schools were crying for good science teachers, and I would hate to think of her giving up. I asked her, if I would provide her with a class set of textbooks, if she would continue to teach for at least another year before making a decision. She was very grateful for my offer, but could not promise she would delay her decision. I had a set of texts sent to her, but became so busy that I failed to follow up with her to see what she had done.

Cal came to work with me in Toledo and to get another donut. During the course of our work, he asked me if I carried an extra car key in my billfold, in case I locked myself out of the car. I told him that I did not and had never locked myself out of the car.

Several months afterward, he flew into Dayton to work with me. I arrived early to meet him, and sat in the car reviewing my call reports for the schools that I planned to take him to. I glanced at my watch and it was time for Cal to arrive. I jumped out of the car and knew instantly I had locked my keys in it.

I went to his arrival gate and when we met, I told him that our conversation in Toledo had jinxed me. He asked why, and I told him what I had done. We were able to get a security guard to help us, and we were soon on our way. I cannot imagine what would have happened if I would have done that with Herb.

We had some great times at our annual sales meetings. I went on a chartered fishing trip one afternoon with a group of sales reps and a few managers. I was on the lower deck fishing at the bow of the boat when a manager from Texas was fishing from the upper deck. He caught a beautiful fish and was reeling it in, and when it was coming to the surface about four feet below the bow of the boat, I saw a three or four feet long barracuda viciously attack his fish and bite it in two. It quickly turned to finish eating the rest of it. I gained a whole new respect for the dangers of swimming in the ocean.

We were at The Breakers in Palm Brach for one of our sales meetings and a group of us were playing golf at the course by the hotel, on our afternoon off. I was riding on the golf cart with Merrill, a rep from Massachusetts, and after hitting my drive, he hit his and it was like many I have hit before. The ball cleared a very high hedge along the right side of the fairway. When we went to look for the ball there was a man standing beside his new pickup truck with the back window broken. We walked up to him and he said: "This is not my day. I was served with divorce papers this morning and now this." Merrill gave him his insurance information to take care of the damage, but never heard from him.

During the summer of 1986 I decided to complete my last semester hour for my degree. I went to the registration office to check my status, and to confirm that I needed only one hour. The counselor suggested that I take a sociology course that was being offered for the summer. He told me to see the professor that was teaching the course to make arrangements for enrollment.

I went to see him, and he told me that he hoped that I was not expecting to attend class each week, because he was teaching students who only needed a course or two to meet their graduation requirement. I told him that I fit into that category and gave him some of my background information.

He instructed me to purchase a particular text-book and read the first four chapters and write a brief outline of them. His second requirement was to pick any other chapter in the text and write a ten page report on it. He then told me to interview a minority person, and write a term paper about the interview. He told me to have all the papers to him within six weeks and that there would be no classes to attend.

It was an interesting assignment. I read the four chapters and completed the outline. I chose to write my short paper about the Native American Indians. What an eye opener. I did quite a bit of research, in addition to reading the chapter in the book. When I was working for The Ohio Brass Company in the shipping department, I packed hardware for the transmission lines that were being built, and the Indians were so desperate for firewood that they would empty the parts out of the crates and use them for their fires.

I interviewed a female doctor who had gone through medical school in the 1950's. In answer to my questions, she discussed with me the difficult time that she had breaking into the essentially all male establishment. I wrote the term paper and called the professor to meet with him to go over my work.

I met with him to discuss my work because I did not want him to think that I had paid someone to do it for me. We had a very good discussion, and I learned that he had worked with the Bureau of Indian Affairs. I received an A for my grade and finally received my degree.

We were at another sales meeting one year and I went to the registration desk about something and one of the reps was in line ahead of asking for a wakeup call for 6:00am. The clerk responded: "Sir, it is already 6:30." Some reps had way too much fun.

During one of the meetings I went with Fred, the sales rep for southern Florida, to a school to make a chemistry presentation for him. When I was finished with my presentation, Fred made a presentation of another program to another group of teachers.

He began his presentation by stating the name of the text and the course that it was to be used for. About three minutes into his presentation one of the teachers interrupted him and said that they were expecting a presentation of a text for another course. Without skipping a beat, Fred did an about face and introduced the same book for the course that was named. He continued as if nothing had happened. Only Fred could get by with such a smooth transition.

As the years passed, our company developed more and more product. Our business plans were requiring more work with far more details and a significant amount of narrative. There were many forms to be filled out which gave management most of the information they required. I began to wonder if anyone was actually reading our business plans. I decided to find out and as I was typing the narrative, I interrupted it and asked if anyone was reading it to call me. I continued the narrative with the question placed in mid sentence and never heard from anyone. My business plans became much easier to do from that time on.

I was working in Cincinnati one year helping Ted with an exhibit when a teacher approached me and asked if our company published a Marine Biology text. I told her that the college division did, but I did not have one with me. I told her that I would be working at another exhibit the following week in Dayton, and if she came to Dayton, I would have one for her. She was anxious to receive it and did not want one mailed to her.

She came to Dayton to see me and pick up the text that I had told her I would have for her. She explained to me that she and her family were going on a year cruise around the world and that there would be a computer on board for her eighth grade son to use to keep up with his studies. She said that he was a gifted student and was very interested in marine biology. I gave the text to her and wished them well on their adventure. About a year later, I received a very nice thank you letter from that young man.

Prentice Hall had been developing a literature program for grades six through twelve. When we attended our winter sales meeting, we received substantial information about it, and provided with presentation binders. I knew immediately that the program would be very successful.

It was a program that was truly revolutionary. I had been identifying potential adoptions for literature, and I followed up with them to make presentations to many teachers using the binders that were provided. With the help of our very competent consultants, I had great success with the program.

I had learned of a very large potential adoption that would take place the following year, and I began seeing as many teachers as I could that would be involved in making the decision to choose what program they wanted. I scheduled one of our consultants to make the presentation. I was working in Indiana at one of their workshops and heard the consultant make her presentation. I was shocked because she had been forced to memorize a script for her presentation.

When I picked her up at the airport the night before she was scheduled to make her presentation, we went to dinner, and I asked her to forget everything that she had memorized and to concentrate on several points that I wanted her to cover. She did exactly what I wanted her to do, and we received the largest order that I had received in my career.

Later that year my good friend and co worker, Ted, was killed in a plane accident.

There was a fellow, whose name was Don, working in our sales service center that was interested in a sales position. Cal was able to have him transferred to the sales position to replace Ted. Don had taught literature for many years and he was very talented. He portrayed Mark Twain for many functions, and we used him often at our workshops. Paul and I enjoyed working with Don.

I purchased Ted's bicycle from Ted's widow, Libby, and asked Paul if he would be interested in going on the Greater Ohio Bicycle Ride in June. It is a

350 mile ride held each year that lasts for one week and covers different parts of the state.

Paul agreed and we decided that we would stay in hotels rather than camping out, as most of the participants do. We met in Oberlin on a Sunday afternoon and road to Fremont. As we were riding the next day, I was several yards in front of Paul as I crossed railroad tracks. I saw that a tire could wedge against the rail and I called back to Paul to warn him. I continued to ride and realized that Paul was not behind me. I saw him walking his bike and went back to see him. He had ruined his tire rim and had taken quite a fall. We were able to have the rim replaced and continued on the ride.

We decided not to stay on the fifty mile per day schedule. We decided to ride eighty or ninety miles one day so that we could complete the ride earlier. As we were riding from Port Clinton to Bucyrus the next day we ran out of water. It was over 90 degrees and we stopped at a farmhouse where there was a girl outside, and we asked her for some water. When we arrived in Bucyrus, the restaurant in the hotel where we were staying was closed. I was exhausted, and grabbed something from the vending machine to eat, before we rode another couple of miles to a restaurant. As I look back on that incident, I believe my exhaustion was a precursor of the diabetes that I would be diagnosed with a year or so later.

I had always wanted to speak with an astronaut and my chance came when Prentice Hall sponsored Colonel Mike Mullane and his wife, Donna, to speak at our state science convention. I was sitting at my desk one morning and the phone rang. When I answered, it was Colonel Mullane calling to request some details about the convention.

He was scheduled to speak on a Saturday morning after the exhibit hours had concluded on Friday evening. He told me that there would be some NASA officials meeting him at the convention, and I offered to host all of them for lunch on Saturday. My wife and I were honored to meet and talk with all of them.

Colonel Mullane spoke about going on a mission, and his wife spoke about what it was like from a wife's perspective, especially the trauma of experiencing delays.

Two or three years after Ted was killed, our national sales meeting was held in La Jolla, California. Paul and I flew together and after we had checked in Paul said: "Lets' go for a walk and get the lay of the land." We began walking on a road that led us to the south end of Torrey Pines golf course.

The end of the road overlooked the ocean which was below a very high cliff leading down to it. I noticed steps going down the side of the cliff and suggested to Paul that we walk down to the ocean. We made it to the shore and after touching the ocean we saw that it was a nude beach. We turned around and climbed the steps up to the road.

Sometime later, I was telling my dentist about the experience and he was familiar with it and told me that it was called Black Beach.

John, a sales rep from Indiana, had a son who was a teaching professional at a golf course in Palm

Springs. John asked me if I would like to stay an extra night when our meeting ended to play golf with them. I wanted to do it but I had a meeting scheduled for the following week and had to return home. I had to prepare for it and could not spare the time for golf.

On Friday evening a group of us went to Coronado after our evening meal. While there, I took a small tour of Hotel Del Coronado and purchased a sweatshirt with the hotel's name on it.

When I arrived home, I wore the sweatshirt and a pair of shorts to Dayton. I was checking in late in the evening and I laid them on the rack above the clothes hanger, which I never did.

The following week I was working in northern Ohio, and I remembered what I had done. I called the hotel to enquire if they were found and was told that they were not there. I moaned so much about losing that shirt that my wife called the Hotel Del Coronado to purchase another one for me.

I am normally an early riser, and while at a couple of sales meetings in Florida, I had breakfast with Darrell, our new manager. He was in a battle with cancer. I got to know him and had much respect for him.

He came to Cincinnati, even though he was not feeling well, to work with Paul and I at one of the conventions. That evening he took us to one of his favorite restaurants known for their ribs. It was also reasonably priced. We had a good time with Darrell and he went back to Indiana the following day.

Paul and I went to a restaurant that was located on top of a building overlooking the city. The food was very good but also very expensive.

When I saw Darrell a few weeks later, I told him that when he left, Paul and I splurged. He replied: "I noticed that." Of course, he was referring to his review of our expense reports.

Later that spring I was asked to work in California for a couple of weeks. I flew to San Francisco and Bob, the manager, had a car packed with samples waiting for me. I met with him and another sales rep for about an hour that Sunday evening and he gave me my assignment. I would be working north of the city, and he gave me general directions.

As I was driving north on the main highway, because of the earthquake that had occurred a year or more earlier, all traffic was diverted unto the city streets. I had no idea where I was, but found a street going north, figuring that it would eventually end at the bridge. As I continued driving, I came to an area where I noticed people lying down in doorways. I thought: "This has to be Haight Asbury that I had read about in the 1960s." A short time later I saw the sign confirming it. It was time to get a street map.

I drove a couple of blocks up the road to a gas station and the attendant asked where I was headed. I told him I was trying to get to the bridge and he told me I had been doing a good job as it was only a few blocks further.

I crossed that beautiful bridge and continued driving to Novato. I checked into a hotel and began to map out my sales calls for the following morning.

I was up about 4:30am to make phone calls to my customers in Ohio before beginning my work in California.

I stayed in Novato for two nights and while there, I called a former Prentice Hall sales rep, Jerry, who was living there. We had dinner one evening and exchanged news on what we were doing. It was good to see him again.

After working out of Novato, I worked my way to Santa Rosa where, I stayed for two nights. I was enjoying calling on the schools, but with trying to handle my Ohio territory at the same time, it was a very long week.

I worked in the Santa Rosa and Napa valley areas for the next two days. My last call for the week was Napa schools and by the time I left Napa High School it was after 3:30pm. I had experienced the shock of driving in that heavy California traffic all week, and I decided that I would really experience it, by returning to the hotel near the airport via crossing the Oakland-San Francisco Bridge during rush hour on a Friday night.

I have never seen anything like it. There were eighteen toll booths and after paying the toll, the traffic light at the booth was blinking red/green so rapidly that you would never know whether you continued on red or green. There were eighteen lanes for over a mile and a half before narrowing to five lanes to cross the bridge. It took me over an hour from the bridge to my hotel that evening. I had a meal and prepared for the trip back to Ohio.

After working in Ohio for a couple of weeks I made another trip to San Francisco to work an area south of the city. I stayed the week at Burlingame. As I recall, I believe that my first sales call that week was in Fremont. I went to a McDonalds for breakfast, after making my sales call at the high school. As I looked around, I think I saw people representing nearly ten or twelve nationalities. What a multiculture city.

On Friday I drove to San Jose to call on the city schools. I was in the very south side of the city, when I made my last call for the day on a very large high school. It again, was after 3:30pm when I walked out of the building.

I had always wanted to see the Monterey Peninsula, and after stopping for a sandwich, I began my drive to see it. When I began the seventeen mile drive, I stopped at the first golf course on the right side of the road. I went to the club house and purchased a ball marker from the Spanish Bay course. I continued my drive to the Spy Glass course and did the same thing. I next stopped at Pebble Beach, and when the clerk at the club house counter told me the price of that small ball marker was fifteen dollars, I decided to have a hamburger in the clubhouse, and he could keep the ball marker.

The drive was every bit as beautiful as I had expected. I completed the drive around the peninsula and drove to Carmel. There was a drive entrance to the beach with a telephone on the beach not far from the ocean. I called Marilyn to let her hear the sounds from the Pacific.

I left Carmel and continued on highway 1, which followed the coastline to Half Moon Bay. The drive is about 100 miles, and as I was driving along looking at the ocean, I notice that I was the only one driving on the highway. It was probably 7:30pm or after by this time, and it was hard to believe that there were thousands of people living several miles away and not one car on this road. All I could think of was a submarine surfacing and shooting at me like the shooting galleries at the amusement parks.

By the time I reached Half Moon Bay, it was nearly dark, for the drive over to Burling Game. I was glad I made that trip.

I returned home, and by the end of the school year, many changes were taking place. John, the private and parochial schools sales rep, had been assigned to a high school rep for eastern Ohio. Paul had been assigned the high school rep for western Ohio. Don was made a middle school rep for eastern Ohio and I was assigned the middle school rep for western Ohio. Paul and I voiced our objections to Darrell, but he told us he could do nothing about it. He told us to work the plan, and that it probably would be changed before too long.

As middle school reps, we had much smaller enrollments and not near the product line that the high school reps had. I felt that I had just received a major cut in compensation. I decided to do as Darrell advised, and to make the most of it.

Don and I, along with the rest of the newly appointed middle school reps, were requested to go to Boulder, Colorado to attend a conference. The purpose for our attendance was to learn more about the philosophy of middle schools.

The conference was scheduled for late July, and I made arrangements for Marilyn and I to spend the prior week at a condo near Winter Park. We had a wonderful week exploring many sights, including Estes Park, Steamboat Springs, and Vail. I fished for trout in four or five streams but did not catch one.

While checking out a golf course, we saw the largest elk that I have ever seen. Marilyn got out of the car to take a picture of it and I called to her because she was getting too close to him. I had read about a lady and her son who had ventured too close to one of them and ended up getting trampled. If I recall correctly, her son died from it.

Marilyn and I enjoyed a trail ride with a group from Prentice Hall before the conference started. I went on another ride later that week, and I saw a big coyote standing on a ridge. I asked the trail guide if he was going to attack us. She replied that she didn't know, because it was the first one she had seen. In talking with her, I learned that she was there working for the summer, and that she was from Ashland, Ohio where I had gone to college.

When the conference was over, Marilyn flew back to Denver and we began our trip home. I had driven to Denver using interstate 70 and I wanted to return via interstate 80. A short time after entering Nebraska, I saw the sign for Cabela's and could not resist stopping. I ended up staying in that store for a couple of hours and had a horrible time finding a hotel, before stopping for the night.

We made it home in time for me to unpack and repack for my trip to our annual sales meeting in New York. It was held at The Sagamore Resort, near Lake George. The conference went well and after returning home, I had unexpected surgery. After recovering, I was finally able to begin work in my new territory.

It became obvious to me, that after making many sales calls, I probably would not come anywhere near to making my assigned sales quota. I made scrupulous notes, about purchases planned for the following year, and expected to do much better in my second year in the territory.

In December of that year Darrell lost his valiant fight with cancer. I felt very bad for his wife and family and felt blessed to have known such a fine individual. He had taught me many things, and I enjoyed hearing about his career in publishing.

Meanwhile Paul's wife had a serious health problem, and he was getting more frustrated with our territory alignments. As I recall, Chuck from the home office, was temporarily assigned as our manager.

I completed the selling season, and I did not come close to making my quota. I worked in my storage area, and stocked up with product, so that I could begin running hard when schools reopened for the next school year.

Early that summer Paul called me and told me he had requested a meeting with the president of Prentice Hall to discuss our territory assignments, and that she was willing to see us. I had nothing to do with the request, but went with him to New Jersey for the meeting.

We arrived at the office and met with the president along with the management team. I had full respect for the decision by management and presented our concerns with that respect. After a short while, I was convinced that no change would be made. I was prepared to begin the selling season as a middle school sales rep, and I suggested to Paul we should accept what is and move on.

I was excused from the room, while Paul continued the discussion. The discussion had become very unpleasant, and on our flight back to Ohio, Paul told me that he was not sure if he would be going to the national sales meeting.

I heard nothing more, and as I was flying to the meeting, there was a stop in Atlanta and Chuck boarded the plane, along with many other people from Prentice Hall.

When we reached cruising altitude, Chuck walked up to me and asked if I would like to be a high school rep again. I told him that would be fine with me, and he gave me no further details.

We arrived at the hotel where the meeting was being held, and Don, the other middle school sales rep for Ohio, introduced me to a sales lady named Michelle and told me that she was the new middle school rep for western Ohio. I was told later in the meeting, that I would be the high school rep for western Ohio, and that Paul was no longer with the company. Remain flexible because you never know where you will land.

John, a sales rep from Indiana, who had worked with Darrell for many years with another company, became our new sales manager. He was very helpful and worked with us as though he was another sales rep. He brought material to our workshops and helped us set up our booths. It was a pleasure working with John.

If I am not mistaken, Michelle and I both made our sales quotas for the year. Michelle did not enjoy sales as much as she thought she would, and was able to get another position within the organization.

John called me and asked me if I knew of anyone that he should interview for Michelle's position. Immediately, Janet came to mind. She had been a teacher and also had been a consultant for many years with another publishing company. She had become a sales rep for that company and now had at least two years sales experience.

I had known the sales rep that she had replaced and knew the other reps with her company. Janet and I, along with a few other reps, had enjoyed lunch together several times when we were working exhibits.

I gave John her phone number and asked him to do all he could to hire her. I then called Janet and told her that I had recommended her to our manager. It worked out far better than I could ever have imagined. Janet is an extremely talented individual and she taught me many things that she had learned from her consulting experience.

Janet and I worked for several years as the western Ohio sales team. We worked exhibits with each other and helped each other with workshops. It was a pleasure working with her and getting to know her family.

I was working an exhibit with John and one of our consultants, Sharon, prior to Janet being hired, and I asked her what I could do to improve our way of working. Immediately she said we should dress up our exhibit booth. John gave her permission to go purchase materials to improve things. Sharon returned a couple of hours later with beautiful quilt like table coverings and a beautiful set of bookends. I thanked her many times, as she truly revolutionized the art of displaying educational materials.

There are times during our careers that decisions are made which upset us. I was not going to include this event in the book, but in the process of putting my writing into print, I have decided that it was just too humorous to leave out.

Three or four years after the merger of Allyn and Bacon with Prentice Hall there was a sales meeting in Florida when many of the sales reps were complaining about low sample budgets.

As the sales year went on, it was nearly impossible to stay within the budget that we had received. A highly creative sales rep wrote a letter in the form of a letter that Popeye would have written. It started: "Me thinks the sample budget is too low." It went on for several paragraphs and if I recall correctly, it was in poetic form. That letter, along with some spinach enclosed with it, was mailed to all the sales reps to mail to upper management, if they agreed with it When our national sales manager became aware of what had been done, the whole management team was furious and probably would have fired the instigator of that letter. It became known as the famous spinach letter. You can imagine how it must have stunk by the time it arrived in New Jersey.

The interesting thing about the event was, it did achieve the desired results, because sample budgets improved.

We had a regional meeting for a couple of nights one summer in Granville, Ohio, before attending the national sales meeting. After the first day of our meeting I joined several reps along with our manager, John, in the basement of the Buxton Inn for refreshments. I was standing near a large square post supporting the floor above, and I noticed a lengthy Cleveland Plain Dealer article, pinned to the pillar describing how haunted the Buxton Inn was.

I asked John, our rep from Bay Village, what room he had been assigned. He was in the most haunted room and I was in the second most haunted room. I asked him the next morning if he slept with the door unlocked. He replied that the window was wide open and the door unlocked!

John was such a great manager and we had fun. We worked hard but enjoyed it to the fullest while working.

Work was becoming more and more demanding, and at times, I was having trouble just keeping the lawn mowed. I found myself doing it on Sunday afternoons. I began saying to myself as I mowed: "There is a condo in my future." I thought that it probably would be in North Carolina sometime after I retired.

My brother in law, Don, had died when he was fifty -two years old, and my sister had taken a trip to Italy with a couple of friends a year or two after he died. Marilyn told me that she would be returning to Dayton soon, and that she would be coming to Mansfield for our father's eightieth birthday. She also said that she would like to see a model of a condo that had been built in a development which was just beginning. I had never told her of my thoughts while mowing, and I knew that she wanted to casually look at the design of the model.

The desk that I had purchased in Toledo was buried with work, but it would have to wait. When we arrived home from church and had lunch, we went to see the model. While going through it, I could visualize my office in the basement. It was a large basement with plenty of room for an extra bedroom and bath. I could visualize the fireplace in the corner beside a door leading out to the common area. A couple of hundred yards behind was a two acre retention pond that would be stocked with fish. I really liked the design of the condo and especially the location that was now available.

I rarely carry a checkbook with me but on that Sunday, March 24, 1998, for some reason, it was in my coat pocket. I would never have very much money in my account, but that day, there was over twelve hundred dollars available. I also thought the construction work was very good. I did not mention my thoughts to Marilyn while the sales lady was explaining some of the details to us. She told us that the builder required 5000 dollars down before he would begin construction. We expressed our appreciation for her time with us, and began walking to the van.

As we opened our doors I said to Marilyn: "Lets' just go back inside and see if we can purchase one." All Marilyn said was: "What?" If she had said: "I want to think about it." I would have opened the door to the van and forgotten it.

We returned to see Patty, the real estate agent, and I told her: "Patty, I am writing a check to the builder for twelve hundred dollars. Take it to him, and tell him that I want a particular unit, and to give me two months notice, before he plans to start construction. If I am able to purchase it, I will, otherwise he may keep the twelve hundred dollars." We in essence left, after I had written the check, with no further conversation.

Prentice Hall was in the process of being sold at the time, and I had no idea whether I would even have a job after the company was sold.

We then went to see my father for his birthday and ate cake and ice cream. We did not mention what I had done. We had not seen my sister for several months, and we enjoyed seeing her again. My brother was also with us for a short time, before he went to work.

On our way home Marilyn said to me: "Since we plan to do this, I will check with the wife of our dentist, who owned many apartments, to see if she has an apartment to move into while we are in the process of selling our home." When Marilyn called her, she responded that there were currently none available, but she expected to have a two bedroom apartment available by June. June was the perfect time for us to move because I would be done traveling by that time.

That June, we moved into a two bedroom apartment that had a swimming pool behind it. We also had access to the tennis facility which they owned. It was very close to a grocery and bank which we could easily walk to. In addition the bike path was only a couple of blocks away. Best of all, my lawn mowing was coming to an end.

We rented our home to a pastor and his wife with the understanding that they would purchase it, after living in it for six months. They ended up not being able to purchase it and after we cleaned it up, we sold it to our neighbor's son and daughter- in- law.

Meanwhile, there were many changes taking place with Prentice Hall. John, our manager, had taken a position in the warehouse to oversee various things to help the sales force. An Illinois sales rep became our manager and he was another very fine manager. He helped me in many ways including authorizing me to find some per diem sales help.

I was coming home from an exhibit in Cincinnati, and I called another sales rep, who had just retired from another company. It was a Friday evening, and I asked Fred if he would be interested in doing some per diem work, for me. He told me that he would like to think about it and asked me to call him on

Monday. I went home and asked God to impress on his heart to join us.

I had known Fred for a number of years, and that he was a very diligent sales rep. He was very quiet but very determined in winning sales for his company. I called him on Monday, and he told me that he would like to work for me. I met with him to give him some catalogs, and to go over what I would like him to do, for me. I knew that I would not have to do anything else for him, because he was honest and fully capable of doing the work. He worked for me several years and did a great job. He was a tremendous help, at a time, when I really needed the help.

Before I contacted Fred, Scott Foresman had been merged with Prentice Hall and changes were made to have three sales reps in Ohio, serving grades six through twelve. John, Janet, and I were given sales territories, and Don secured a librarian job with a school district, not far from his home.

I began working very hard in my new territory and quickly learned of two potentially large adoptions, which would be made in the spring.

I also learned that a social studies department head from one of the Toledo area schools was planning to retire. I had known Skip for a number of years, and I contacted him to see if he had any interest in doing some per diem work, for me. He told me that he definitely would be interested in doing some work for me. He was fully knowledgeable about the Prentice Hall social studies product, and it was just a matter of him becoming familiar with the rest of our product. I met with him, and went over our catalogs with him, and the work that I would like him to do for me.

I had positioned myself with two very good per diem sales reps and knew about two potentially large adoptions, that I could concentrate working on. I felt very good about the sales year.

I did not have that good of sales year, the year before, and was not surprised when a regional vice president called me and wanted to meet with me. I had known Martinez for a number of years, and when I answered the phone and heard his voice, I said: "Martinez, you are calling me. I must be on the hit list again." He said: "Yes, I'm the bad boy. Are you able to meet me at the Cleveland airport next week?"

I met him at the airport, and as he was walking up the ramp to meet me, he asked: Are you going to meet your quota this year?" I responded that I had no idea, because I again, was in another territory with another merger that had taken place, and I concluded by telling him to just fire me if I did not make my quota. By that time, all of the sales reps had been through well over a dozen years of raise the quotas and cut the commission programs. I put the results in the Lord's hands, and was planning to put full effort into my work.

We went to lunch, and I gave him some information that he needed, and never heard from him again. I liked Martinez very much, and because of my marketing background with Ohio Brass Company, I knew what he had to do.

By the time the year ended and all sales were totaled, I exceeded my quota by twenty-two per cent. It was, by far, the best year that I had in my career.

Fred and Skip had worked very hard for me, and I had used all the resources available to do the job. I probably used three or four different consultants, to make presentations for me, and they did a traffic job. It was a total team effort.

I ended up making the President's Club and won a trip to London for Marilyn and myself. What a blessing from the Lord that was. When we arrived in London, we met with the other award winners, and were given an itinerary. Marilyn and I took a short nap, because we had flown during the night. We got up and caught one of the famed double decked buses and rode to St. Paul's Cathedral, where I climbed to the top.

We crammed many activities into our short trip, in addition to attending a couple of meetings. We toured the Tower of London, saw Leed's Castle on our way to White Cliffs of Dover, watched changing of the guards, and Marilyn and I rode on The Eye of London, overlooking the city. It was a very enjoyable and enlightening time.

Marilyn and I stayed a couple of extra days to travel to Scotland by train. When we arrived in Edinburgh, we took a walking tour of the city, and returned to London the following day. While we were waiting for the train in Waverly station, I purchased a small bagpipe for my brother. He was a trinket person, and I thought he would like it. After we gave it to him Marilyn would call him, and he would respond by squeezing it, to make it play some kind of music.

After Ted was killed, I began driving to many of our sales meetings. I stopped to see Herb, in Fort Lauderdale one year, and it happened to be his eightieth birthday. His wife had died and he had married her caregiver. We had a great visit. On another trip, I had dinner with Al and his wife at Fort Pierce, and it was another great visit. I am glad that I stopped to see them, because both of them had such a positive influence on me.

When the meetings were over, I, many times would have Marilyn fly to meet me, and we would spend a week visiting friends and relatives on our way back to Ohio.

John, my manager with Prentice Hall, had retired and he and his wife had moved to Sarasota. Marilyn and I stopped to see them, and I played golf with him and another retired sales rep from Ph who also was in Sarasota. During our time together, both Ziggy and John stated that they wished that they had retired earlier than they had.

I was enjoying my work and had not thought much about retiring. We discussed the topic some more and each of them told me that I would know when it was time to retire.

Things had been going very well for Marilyn and I, and I was thankful. We had a special speaker for church services one morning. His name was Russ, whose wife had been battling cancer. We had known them for years. He was retired from teaching Bible classes at our local Christian High School.

I don't remember anything about his message that morning, but I do remember him stopping abruptly to say: "I don't believe anyone will ever really be used by God until they have been severely tested." We were attending services regularly and were involved with things. I also was helping with lawn work but wanted to do more. I had been thinking about writing this book for many years, but I needed to experience more, before I could write it. That morning I asked the Lord to test me, because I wanted to be used of him for his glory.

Our manager, Patrick, had been promoted to regional vice president and Kevin, a sales rep from Illinois, became our manager. Soon changes were made and Rita, also from Illinois, became our manager. She was followed by Bob from Wisconsin, and I was beginning to think that I was too hard to manage. Each of them were very good managers and I liked them very much. PH was growing very fast and management was trying to get people in the right place for the task at hand.

Over the course of my sales career I have enjoyed many fine meals with many beautiful people, but I must tell you about two of them before concluding this chapter.

Patrick was having a regional meeting in Chicago which included many sales reps from several states. We were at a very fine restaurant one evening, and when the waiter had finished taking our meal orders, Patrick ordered a couple of plates of crab legs for appetizers. John, our sales rep from Cleveland, and I were sitting across from one another at the end of a fairly long table. Everyone was involved in conversation when the waiter arrived with the crab legs. John told him to set the plates in front of us. John and I began immediately to have some. About twenty minutes later Patrick asked where the crab legs were. John and I had eaten them! He never said a word as he ordered a couple more plates for the other reps.

I had ridden with Janet to another meeting in Chicago, or possibly the one mentioned above, and the meeting ended about mid afternoon. When we left, she mentioned that she would like to make it to South Bend before stopping for dinner.

I told her that if we were going to do that, I would really appreciate seeing the campus of Notre Dame. We ended up eating at the restaurant on campus. It was very busy and it was the night before the Michigan -Notre Dame Football game. I will never forget the serenity of the waitresses that evening, and the meal was outstanding.

Janet had done some consulting work with teachers or student teachers at the campus and was very familiar with it. We went to the bookstore, after our meal, and it was like a full blown department store.

We then went to see the famous dome, and while walking to it, I noticed many students with heavy backpacks of books on their backs, riding to the library. I said to Janet: "Seeing this gives me hope for our country."

The years after returning from London had gone by very quickly, and Rita was a very good manager. We were informed at the national meeting that summer, of more changes. Rita was reassigned, and another sales rep from California, who had been promoted as a manager for another territory, was to be our manager. In addition, our sales territories were being realigned.

By that time, we also had a lot of technology that accompanied our programs. Mark, our new manager, had worked with me several times, and because of his inexperience, would ask many detailed questions that would never have been asked by a more mature manager.

I was working in Toledo the last part of October, and had a room full of teachers with a consultant, who would be going over our technology product with them. After he began, I went to the car to make some phone calls, and when I checked my voice mail, there was a message from Mark to call him. The way it sounded, I thought that Marilyn had been in an accident or something.

Things were very hectic at this time of year, as teachers were calling, and sending e-mails to request samples, or needed help in obtaining teacher material. The previous night I had sixty or more e-mail requests, in addition to the many voice mails, and Mark wanted me to call him immediately.

When I returned the call, it was certainly nothing that needed to be addressed as the urgency that he had implied. I got a little upset with him, and hung up the phone.

I called Marilyn that evening and told her I thought it was time for me to retire. I was not going to continue working and getting upset so easily.

I told her that I would be making arrangements to go to our timeshare in Pennsylvania, for the weekend, and that I planned to play some golf and pray about the matter.

I called Mark on Monday to inform him of my decision.

Patrick called me to say that he had moved my retirement date to January 15, to allow me to collect vacation compensation. He also asked if I was planning to come to the regional meeting and I told him that I would prefer to attend the summer sales meeting. He was pleased that I would do that.

I worked as a per diem sales rep after I retired. I also made a strong recommendation for another sales rep from another company to replace me. Michelle became my replacement and I was happy for her.

Retirement

He hath showed thee, o man, what is good:
and what doth the Lord require of thee, but
to do justly, and to love mercy, and to walk
humbly with thy God?

Micah: 6:8

After retiring, I continued to work as a per diem sales rep for Michelle. She and Mark came to our home to pick up sales records and to discuss what needed to be accomplished that spring. It was a good meeting with them

I did not waste any time trying to adjust to retirement. Marilyn and I went to Peak and Peek ski resort near Jamestown, New York. I enjoyed the skiing and Marilyn enjoyed the swimming pool and hot tub.

We followed that trip by making another one to Shreveport, Louisiana to see Virginia, a retired doctor, who had employed Marilyn as her office manager and nurse for over seventeen years. The doctor was in an assisted care facility near one of her sons.

From there we went to Norman, Oklahoma to see Karen and her husband Mark. Prior to their marriage, Mark had been in a tragic bicycle accident, and was completely paralyzed with the exception of being able to move three fingers which allowed him to operate his wheel chair. His body had been severely crippled, but his mind was very sharp. I enjoyed getting to know him, and when I get discouraged, I often think of Mark and the uplifting attitude he had. We went to church on Sunday with Mark and Karen, and enjoyed lunch with them, before leaving for a timeshare in Arkansas. We had a great time for the week and we returned home. I worked a few more days for Michelle, before giving our garage a good cleaning.

We had a neighbor whose wife had passed away while they were at their cabin in Canada. Another friend of ours, John, and I made a trip to Canada to see Kenny. His cabin was on the Trent Severn Waterway.

John and I arrived in the evening and it was quite cool. We went to dinner and the next morning, after our breakfast, Kenny took us fishing with his pontoon boat. Kenny caught a very nice fish; John and I had a good time.

Upon returning to the dock in that very swift current, John was standing in the front of the boat as Kenny tried to steer it close to the dock. He hit the dock, as he was turning the boat, and John went flying onto the dock, grabbing the flag pole that was attached to the dock, thus preventing him from going into Kenny's other boat or into the icy water. All Kenny said was: "John, you bent my flagpole."

We had a great time with Kenny and we eventually caught some fish.

A few weeks after my Canadian trip Marilyn and I went to our timeshare in Pennsylvania for a week. I enjoyed the golf and Marilyn kept busy going to craft shows. We returned home for another week or two, and headed for Michigan to spend a few days at our favorite spot, before heading to Florida for my last sales meeting.

I cannot say enough about how well we were treated by Prentice Hall management and my former colleagues. When we entered our room, there were flowers, along with several other gifts. I enjoyed lunch with management, other retirees, and award winners. I participated in some of the training sessions, while Marilyn enjoyed the pool. Time passed very quickly, and it was time for the awards banquet.

It was Friday evening July 24, 2004, at the Fairmont, Turnberry Isle Resort Club, in Aventura, Florida, when I stepped to the podium, in that vast ballroom, looking out to one hundred fifty people, or more, sitting at round tables, to give my fair well address.

As I looked out to that audience dressed in beautiful attire, I was totally amazed at what God had done for me, since that July day in 1959. I thanked management, consultants, and fellow sales reps for helping me through the years. I also told at least one story about textbook sales.

I then told that large audience that I had one last story to tell them. I told them of my being a drunk and hitting myself with that jackhammer, and how

I called out to God with my requests for a faithful wife, a college education, and a job like one those people that I had seen riding in air conditioned automobiles. I told of the vision that I had seen and the question that was posed to me.

I then pointed to my wife, and told them we had been married 42 years, and that with her help, I obtained my college degree. I then told them, that for the last 30 years, I had been riding around in air conditioned cars, calling on schools. I concluded, by pointing my hand at them, and telling them, that they were the full audience that I had seen part of, 45 years ago nearly to the day!

I was presented with a gold watch that evening and after breakfast the next morning, I said goodbye to a number of people. Marilyn and I then departed to go to Key West for the wedding of my friend Ted's youngest son.

It was a beautiful outdoor wedding, and we met many people for the first time. As we were talking Ted's nephew, Jeff, approached us. I had not seen him, since Ted and I had dinner with him in Naples. He had been in Europe teaching golf for the last several years. He was now working at a very exclusive golf club in Naples. He invited Marilyn and I to meet him at the course, so that I could play a round of golf with him. We did, and Marilyn and I rode on a cart with Jeff on the other one, and we enjoyed seeing the development while I played golf with Jeff. It was so good to see Jeff again along with seeing Ted's family.

Marilyn and I visited several friends and relatives on our trip home for more retirement living. That fall, we made several more short trips and continued to do so for several years. One time when I went to the Post Office to have our mail held, the clerk said to me: "You are gone more than anyone I know."

She was probably right. For the past 30 years I had probably slept alone in hotel beds for seven and a half years. Marilyn and I were making up for it.

I had always wanted a pontoon boat and a small sail boat. I purchased a used pontoon boat and also found a used sailboat for four hundred dollars.

My friend Jim helped me to assemble the sailboat, and we enjoyed sailing many times on a nearby lake. Marilyn and our family and friends also enjoyed the pontoon boat.

Since our first trip to Beulah in 1969, I had always wanted to sail on Crystal Lake with Jim. We made two trips to that lake and had the time of our lives. Sailing on that crystal clear lake in two foot waves was a sailor's dream for me.

Jim's brother was living on a large sailboat docked at Marina Del Rey in California. Jim and I flew out to see him, and we sailed to Catalina Island. It was Ben's first trip to the island without a crew member, and he was carefully watching his instruments, as the fog began to set over the ocean when we were approaching the island. I saw a big sigh of relief when we saw the island.

We stayed in Two Harbors for the night and sailed south to Avalon the next day. I remembered Guy Lombardo's New Years eve dance band performances from the 40's and had always wanted to see Avalon. Another small wish had been granted by our loving Father.

We had our friends Jim and Dixie, John and Nancy, John and Debbie, and Toni and Terry over to Pennsylvania with us at one time or another and Terry and Toni had been to Michigan with us at least twice. Marilyn and I had also been to Dallas to see our former neighbor's daughter Melanie, and she had given us the tour of the city.

I was working as a per diem sales rep, helping with the lawn at church, helping neighbors, and really enjoyed being retired. I was also asked to be a board member for our condominium association and was serving in that capacity.

Marilyn and I had enjoyed this mix of work and pleasure for several years, but it is unreasonable to expect it to continue for the rest of our lives. The test that I asked the Lord for was about to begin.

The Test

"God whispers to us in our pleasures, speaks to us in our conscience, but shouts to us in our pain. It is his megaphone to a deaf world."

C.S. Lewis

Within four years after retiring I had done virtually all that I really wanted to do. In addition to all the things that Marilyn and I had enjoyed, we went on a very relaxing cruise in the Caribbean.

I had taken a general investment course in college that was taught by a former stock broker. It had been very interesting to me and now that I was retired, I began an education journey like Captain Ahez, of Moby Dick's fame, as he pursued that great white whale.

I went to seminar after seminar, on different types of investing and stock and option trading. I read numerous books and subscribed to many investment publications. I have never studied as much in my life, and the expense soon exceeded more than I had spent obtaining my four degree.

I had set a very high financial target, for the purpose of providing funds for various organizations to use in their quest to provide needs for people, and lead them to the knowledge of Christ.

Had I followed my first instinct, I would have reached that goal in a relatively short period of time. A very conservative investment advisor had written in his publication about a company that he would not normally recommend, but, because of the high profile stores selling their product, he suggested that his readers might consider investing a small amount in their stock. Had I invested 50,000 dollars with them and played golf, it would have soon reached more than the goal I had set.

Instead, I wanted to become a very knowledgeable investor and stock trader. By the time the financial crisis of 2008 hit, I had exhausted nearly all of the funds that I had accumulated throughout my working career.

We had used some to travel, of course, and I had helped our grandson and daughter with their needs.

My per diem work was no longer required, further exasperating the situation. I had, for the most part, achieved every goal that I had set for myself. I had never put so much effort into trying to achieve something, and totally failed like this before.

As I was assessing our situation, I was reading: "Our Daily Bread" on November 19, 2008. At the bottom of the narrative there was this statement: "Facing an impossibility gives us the opportunity to trust God."

Many of us, if not most of us, spend a lifetime trying to build a ship, to sail on the sea of tranquility during our retirement years.

Eventually all of us will experience the stormy seas, and someone will have to began the dismantlement of that ship, no matter what its' size.

Jim and I had sailed on that beautiful lake in Michigan and I no longer had the desire to sail in muddy waters. In July of 2007, Marilyn and I took the sailboat to Michigan, and after I had sailed, I took it to the marina and gave it to one of the workers.

In August of 2008, I sold our pontoon boat to further reduce expenses. We had enjoyed it, but the luster had worn off.

I had purchased several timeshare weeks and began transferring ownership to our children, which I was planning to do at some point in time, only not quite this soon.

Financial adversity continued to the point that I finally had to assess Marilyn of our situation. She immediately found employment and I soon had a part time job. Later, we both were working part time for the same business.

We were making progress, but the test was far from over. I had to continue reminding myself that I had asked for a test to prepare me to be used by God in some significant way.

The apex arrived in 2012 when we experienced some of the highest highs and the lowest lows possible. It began on January 1 when the general I mentioned earlier in this book died. On March 6, our long time good friend and former neighbor suddenly died on his morning walk.

Our 50th wedding anniversary was on March 9th but, because of not wanting to contend with possible weather problems, our children planned a reception for us in April. It was held at our church and we had a wonderful time.

Our good friend Karen visited us for a few days in July. I called Janet and her husband Don, along with Don and his wife Margaret, to come to a picnic at our home for a mini PH reunion. I also called John and his wife Maggie to join us.

I had not spoken to John since I had retired, and we had a very good conversation. They were not able to join us for the good time. He died suddenly on August 4th.

Another PH sales rep and manager, Wendell, who I mentioned earlier died in August.

In October, we hosted a reception for Marilyn's 50 year reunion of her nursing class. We had another wonderful time with them.

On November 26 exactly twenty-three years after the death of my good friend Ted's death, our forty-eight year old daughter, Tamara, was found dead by our mentally challenged granddaughter.

Death was not over. The son of our former neighbors died in December. He was about the same age as our daughter. That was followed later that month, by the sudden death of Marilyn's cousin, who was married to the sister of our neighbor.

As I thought about all that had transpired, I thanked the Lord for preparing me to face this trial, through the reading of his word many times. My trial, with the exception of the death of our daughter, has been nothing compared to the challenge that Mark suffered.

Going through trials, develop in us a complete trust in God, which you cannot learn in any other way. He does indeed provide as he promised.

Contentment

But my God shall supply all your need according to his riches in glory by Christ Jesus.
Philippians 4:19

Not that I speak in respect of want: for I have learned, in whatsoever state I am, therewith to be content.

Phil. 4:11

I had several plaques hanging on the wall in my office and two small trophies on a shelf. I had received one of them for being on the right team for golf. {I am not that good.} The other one was for coming in second in an all day church softball tournament while playing on the same team with our son, when I was 50 years old.

I gathered them all up and threw them in the trash. I wanted nothing in my office to call attention to myself. I was not bitter with God but rather had grown much closer to him by having gone through all that we had faced.

I had a box full of athletic letters and awards along with a beautiful scrapbook that had been put together by the mother of a member on our football team. At my wife's urging, I gave the box to our son. This was my last dismantlement.

My burning desire for whatever I wanted was now extinguished. It was time to write this book that had been on my mind for years.

In 2006, Janelle, a teacher from our high school, organized a reunion for the members of the 1956 football team that had posted an undefeated season. It was a wonderful time. We enjoyed a meal, and we were honored at half time of one of the games that year. I had not seen most of the players since I had graduated.

Ray, our former quarterback, and I have become quite close again, and we call each other several time a year.

Dayton, one of the managers of that team, took it upon himself to have Ray and I inducted into the Plymouth-Shiloh Distinguished Hall of Fame. We were honored by school officials, and presented with plaques during the half time of one of the basketball games in December 2013.

I decided to hang that plaque above my desk to spur me on to write this book. I was sitting in my chair reading one morning and glanced at that plaque and thought: "Lord that is nice, but has my life really affected anyone?" Three days later, I received a note from one of the boys that we had taken on a trip to Pennsylvania many years ago. He told me that I may have achieved much in Plymouth, but that I had been an influence on his life, which was far more important to him. That note is one of my prized possessions. Thank You Marty!

Several years ago a new couple moved into our condo development and Marilyn and I have become good friends with them. Both are active in our condo association. Barb is on the social committee and Jerry helps me maintain the pond behind our unit.

Jerry is also a skier and last fall he asked me if I plan to ski this year. I told him that I would not be skiing until I had completed a book that I planned to write. He then asked if his name would be in it. I told him if he agreed to play at least one round of golf with me, I would try to do that. He agreed, and I am holding him to it.

Does being content, mean that I have no goals? No, I still have quite a few things that I would like to accomplish.

If the rapture of the true church does not occur first, I would like for my life to end as it did for my father-in-law and for Harry James.

My father-in-law sold his last car on a Thursday or Friday before Marilyn and I took him to the hospital on Monday. He died on Wednesday.

Harry James gave his last concert on June 26, 1993 and died nine days later.

Epilogue

I have travelled well over two million miles since that special gift was given to me nearly fifty-seven years ago. It remains packed as I use it every day.

My father-in-law was trying to learn something new every day right up to his death. I hope to do the same.

I have read hundreds of books and I have attended many, many seminars over my lifetime. I have heard speeches from people with probably the most intellect of any on this planet. But none compares with the most profound advice I heard from an eight year old boy, using just four words.

Marilyn and I were driving to work one morning several years ago, and she had called a lady with a son, who was living with our daughter.

It was early in the morning and her son, Liam, was ready for school. I asked Marilyn to ask Liam: "What's the good word for today?"

In less than a minute, he replied: "Don't fight the truth."

I am the way, the truth, and the life: no man cometh to the Father but by me.
                    The Lord Jesus Christ John 14:6

Decision

Behold I stand at the door, and knock: If any man hear my voice, and open the door, I will come in to him, and will sup with him, and he with me.

Revelation 3:16

In the book of Luke chapter 23 verses 27 through 45, the crucifixion of Christ is described along with the two thieves. One thief remained an unbeliever while the other acknowledged his sin and deserved punishment. He then turned to Jesus in full trust and asked to be remembered or pardoned for his sin. Jesus responded by telling him that: "Today he would be with Him in paradise."

Several years ago on a Saturday night or early Sunday morning, we received a call from the woman who was living with my Aunt. She told us that she had taken my Aunt to the hospital and that she did not expect her to live long. I felt an immediate urge to go to Florida. Sunday after church, we left for Winter Garden.

We arrived on Monday evening and went to the hospital to see her. She was full of confidence that she would live. By Wednesday evening she realized that her death was very near and she exclaimed: "I am not ready for this. My mother read her Bible and went to church but I tried to read it and could not understand anything I read."

My wife stayed with her that night and showed her verses in scripture where we are promised salvation by doing just two things. We must acknowledge our sin and ask for forgiveness from Jesus. She did that, and the peace of God was very evident until she died the next day.

Generally new converts to the Faith are encouraged to attend a Bible believing church and begin reading scripture. My Aunt expressed her frustration of having tried to read the scripture, not knowing where to begin. I suspect that there are many others who have experienced the same thing.

If all you do, as I did for many years, is attend church and read a few verses of scripture a day, your faith will remain weak. When I began to mine the gold of scripture, my faith grew. I would like to suggest a way to begin reading your bible. I have never heard any minister or anyone else suggest this, but after I had read many versions of the Bible several times, I found that reading the book of John through in one setting, and also reading the book of Acts through in one setting, increased my faith tremendously.

The book of John contains some of the most intimate discussions that Jesus had with his disciples before being betrayed. The book of Acts records the activities of his disciples as the church was being established.

Fifty some years later, after seeing that pastor hold his Bible up, and telling what a gold mine it is, I am beginning to understand what he meant. The more you mine, the more nuggets you find.

My Wife

***Whoso findeth a wife findeth a good thing,
and obtaineth favor of the Lord.***

Proverbs 19:22

Most of this book has been about how the Lord worked to give me what I had requested of him. However, he worked through my wife to do it.

Throughout our lives, her sole love has been to the Lord first. Then she would do whatever it took to please me. She has stood behind me in everything that I have undertaken. Her life has been characterized by one word. Serve!

If a journal had been kept, I would guess we have had more meals interrupted by a request from someone, for Marilyn's advice, than we have enjoyed without such requests.

I never objected to her helping someone because she loves what she is doing, and encourages me to do the same.

I was so pleased to see her learn to play bridge, as she had always wanted to do, but I never knew about it, until we moved to our condo. It is one of the rare things that she does for her own enjoyment

Whenever I look at my hands, I am reminded of how I have been blessed. A faithful wife, and with her help, I received a college education, and she allowed me to work for a company in a job, which I truly enjoyed.

The Lord blessed us with three children, and she did a wonderful job of providing for their needs, while I was away.

Jim, our oldest, knew what he wanted to do before he was in high school. He studied electronics and became a software design engineer. He married our neighbor's daughter, Midge, and they had two daughters. Kristin and Jamie are now grown, and working. Marilyn and I have enjoyed several vacations with them, and have seen many things, that our daughter-in-law arranged for us.

Our daughter, Tamara, made some decisions that did not work out very well for her. She did, however, raise a son, Alex, who has done very well. She also did a great job of preparing our granddaughter, Amanda, who has special needs, to live in a group home with two other young women. We are thankful for this, as Tammy died before her fiftieth birthday.

Our other daughter, Jennifer, has done very well. She followed her brother in the computer field, except that she works to keep the computers working functioning. She owns a home, and has a lady, Lora, with two boys, Liam and Tigan, living with her.

I could not ask for better children. All of them have kept in touch with us and we have many good times with them. I am most grateful that they have remained active in church throughout their lives.

Educators

I have enjoyed the opportunity to have worked in sixteen states, by working at conventions, or calling on teachers and administrators of our schools.

While making thousands of sales calls, I have learned of the extra effort put forth by teachers and supervisors, such as Ms Day, from Dayton, for our nation's students.

I took three supervisors to lunch before I retired, to let them know of my plans. One of them asked what I planned to do when I retired, and I told them of my desire to write this book.

As Cheryl, Dorothy, Janice, and I got up to leave, Cheryl said: "Lets' say a prayer for Larry."

As Cheryl began to pray, I thought we had entered the throne room of God himself. I have never heard such a fervent prayer before, and it was for me. I have read of such a prayer, which was given by General Howard during the Civil War on behalf of Major E. M. Hill, when he refused to give him leave, because of the work that needed to be done during a very critical time of the war. It is recorded in the book, by Major Hill's wife:

Mrs. Hills' Journal Civil War Reminiscences

If this book is read by anyone, it will be the result of that prayer given by Cheryl, on that day in December 2003.

Thank You, Cheryl

Preserved for a Purpose

For He shall give his angels charge over thee to keep thee in all thy ways.

Psalms 91:11

Rat Poison
Yellow Jacket Bees
Stabbed by a Pitchfork
Potential Vehicle Accidents
Lawn Mower Miracle
Plane Rides
Out of Body Experience

Rat Poison

There have been numerous times in my life, when the Lord has chosen to protect me from probable tragedy. One time happened, when, I was three or four years old.

I rose from bed and ventured to the kitchen, where, I noticed a piece of bread laying on the floor. It had something red on it which, I thought was catsup. I put it into my mouth and detected a funny taste, and somewhat hot. I don't know if I swallowed it or not, but, I woke my mother, to ask her what it was.

She told me that it was rat poison, and I told her that I may have eaten some of it. She called the doctor, and he rushed to our house and immediately began pumping my stomach.

Yellow Jacket Bees

I was probably six years old, on a hot summer day, when I asked my mother to allow me to sell some lemonade. She made a pitcher of it for me, and I took it to the front sidewalk, and set it down on a wooden crate with some cups. I don't remember actually selling, any but it sure was good.

I was ready to try again, the next day, but could not find the wooden crate to sit the pitcher on. I went to the backyard and saw it near a bush. As I walked closer to it, I saw some bees on it. I picked up a stick to move it, and the bees came after me. They chased me, as I was running to the house, and by the time I made it into the house, I had been stung twelve or fourteen times.

I not only was hurting from being stung but was very angry with my neighbor, because I was sure that he had thrown the crate near the bees nest. When I encountered him the next day, he was trying to run up the stairs next to a concrete wall. He gave a good fake, and I slammed my fist into the wall.

I am very glad that I did not hit him. He turned out to be one of the best quarterbacks, on any team that ever played for our high school.

Stabbed by a Pitchfork

My friend Jim and I worked several years for a local farmer, while we were in junior high school.

One day, the owner gave each of us a pitchfork and asked us to clean out the barn. The manure was packed down and was very hard. It also was the first time that we had worked with a pitchfork. Things were going very well, and we were making good progress with filling the wagon.

After a short break, we began working, not paying attention to how close we were. Jim was behind me when, his pitchfork slipped on the hard surface. A tong entered my shoe on the right back side, going directly into my heel, about an inch or more.

I took off my shoe and sock; it had entered my foot below the ankle. I squeezed some blood out, and we continued working.

We did not tell anyone about the incident. When I got home, I put some salve on the wound, and it healed without complications.

Potential Vehicle Accidents

There have been numerous times in my over 2 million miles of travel, either as a passenger or driver of a motor vehicle, that I have been divinely protected from injury or a fatality. I will tell about 3 of them.

While in high school, a group of us went to Sandusky for some reason, which I don't remember. On the way home that late night, the driver was speeding, and when he approached an underpass, he passed on the left side of the supporting pillar, while we were going uphill.

When I was working in construction work, I was riding in a dump truck in pouring down rain in very heavy traffic. We were on our way to a job site. All of a sudden, we began making a 360 degree turn in slow motion, while we were going 50 or 60 miles per hour. There were cars all around us, but we did not hit any of them. I said: "Great job, Kenny."

When I was working for CEBCO, I had several book exhibits in Michigan on Saturdays. Each October I attended the Detroit Area Science Exhibit and almost all of them were held on a beautiful sun shinny, and very warm day.

On the way home after exiting interstate 75 onto route 23 south, the traffic would slow down. Many times there would be a mile or more between my car and the truck ahead of me. I don't remember when I began, but sometimes, I would lock the steering wheel between my knees and take a cat nap.

I fell sound asleep one time and woke up going 70 miles per hour when the speed limit was 55 miles per hour. I was about to go under the truck, that had been more than a mile ahead of me, when I fell asleep! I immediately turned left to pass the truck, and I'm quite sure my right fender went under the trailer of the truck. At the same time, I saw a state highway patrolman coming from the median to pull me over.

I pulled over and told him to write the ticket because I was happy to be alive.

Needless to say, whenever I am feeling sleepy while driving, I get out and walk around.

Lawn Mower Miracle

Sometime during my early twenties, a planters' wart appeared on the bottom of my right heel. During my time in Texas for Air National Guard training, all of the marching required began to cause it to bother me. When I came home, I let it go for several years and it continued to grow larger. I had tried the usual burying a penny treatment and other such treatments without success.

I went to a podiatrist and he began a series of dry ice treatments, which, were very painful and did not achieve the desired results. I discontinued that treatment, and it became more and more painful when I walked. I even had shooting pain in my leg that reached my knee. I decided to check with a surgeon.

Marilyn was working at the hospital and she asked one of the leading surgeons, in the area about it. After listening to her, explain the problem, he told her that he would not try to remove it, for fear that I possibly, would have to have my leg amputated.

Several months went by, and I began to ask the great Physician to take care of it. After praying about it for several months, He took care of it, in a way that was miraculous.

I was mowing lawn at our church for the first time, using a mower that one of the members brought from his home. He showed me how to operate it. It had a steel plate three or four inches thick, and about a foot wide by thirty or more inches long, hanging from the frame directly behind the rear wheels. The mower weighed well over twelve hundred pounds with that plate steel hanging on it.

I got on the mower and made my first trip around the perimeter of the lawn. As I was going up a hill, the mower lost some traction, and the front of the mower came up a little. It was a fairly large lawn and as I was coming down the hill, I thought to myself: "I wonder if that mower fell on top of me, would I survive?"

It did not take long until I had an answer to my question. As I was going up the hill, the mower began to buck, and because I was not familiar enough with the mower, to step on the break or let up on the gas pedal, it turned completely over. I fell off the seat, landing on the ground, lying on my back with my feet pointing uphill toward the mower. I did not think that I had time to get away from it as it fell.

As the mower cleared the ground falling toward me, I raised my knee and the seat of the mower hit it, breaking the fall somewhat. The steering wheel hit my chest and bounced off. The mower ended up with the steering wheel landing on my right leg just below my knee. The seat had my other leg pinned to the ground. The mower continued to run, even though it was upside down.

As I was trying to get my breath, I was pinned to the ground for several minutes. I finally managed to free my left leg and was able to push the seat enough to free my right leg.

When I was able to get up, I began to take deep breaths because I felt like my left lung was collapsed. I felt no sharp pain and was sure I had not broken any bones.

Because the mower had continued to run, no one in the church suspected anything was wrong. When I went in to tell what happened, one of the men insisted I go to the hospital to be checked. He called an ambulance to take me. The medical staff checked me and told me that I would be fine when the soreness was gone.

Several months after that incident, I was sitting at my desk at work and realized I was not in pain from that wart. I took off my shoe and sock and there was no sign of it!

I told Marilyn about it being gone. She told the surgeon about it and the first question he asked was: "Did he receive a blow to his leg?" When she told me what he had said, I thought back to that lawn mower accident. I have not had a wart since that time.

Our God is an awesome God, and He sometimes works in very mysterious ways.

Plane Rides

I have traveled thousands of miles via airplanes and all but two have been routine. The two described below deserve mention of God's divine protection.

My first ride took place in October of 1962. I was riding in an Air Force plane, along with about twenty-four or twenty-five other airmen, bound for basic training in San Antonio. There was one, possibly two pilots on board, and we were told to strap ourselves to the wall of the fuselage of the plane. We were seated on benches on each side with a small isle running down the middle.

We had left from Columbus and all was going well, until the pilot told us that we would be making a stop in Lake Charles to have an oil leak checked. As we were flying somewhere over Louisiana, the plane suddenly dropped, and my head nearly hit the ceiling because I had loosened the strap to the side of the plane.

We continued to experience turbulence and were bouncing all over the sky. Young airmen all over the aircraft began to fill their barf bags. The plane soon stunk worst than a garbage truck as we continued to bounce. I was eating a sandwich, and the airman setting diagonally across from me, was also eating one. We did not get sick but all, if not most of the others, did.

We finally landed at Lake Charles. The pilot opened the door to the cockpit and exclaimed: "Whew, kind of rough up there wasn't it boys."

My second most memorable ride happened several years after my ANG ride. We were visiting Marilyn's cousin and his family after Thanksgiving one year and our six or seven year old daughter asked her cousin Luther to take us for a plane ride. Luther had his own crop dusting business and was also a pilot instructor.

It surprised me that she wanted to do that since she had never been in a plane. She was also younger than her brother. When she asked for the second time, Luther said: "OK, let's go."

Our two children climbed into the back seat of the plane and fastened themselves with their seat belts. I got in beside Luther. He had two runways on the farm. One was an east/west runway and the other was north/south. Because of the wind direction, he lined the plane up to take off going east. As he continued to carefully watch the wind sock for a few minutes, he changed our position to take off going north.

He waited a few minutes and committed to take off. As we were going down the runway, the wind reversed direction, and we had no lift! At the end of the runway there was an elevated road in front of us with utility lines on poles which gave very little clearance between the road and the lines.

He said: "Hold on, we are going to fly under the lines." I sat there calmly, thinking that he did it all the time, and I was not concerned. As we reached the end of the runway, there was enough lift for us to clear the road, which I had looked at, to see if any cars were coming. As the nose of the plane began crossing the road, he dipped the tail to avoid hitting the wires with it.

We were approaching a wooded area on the other side of the road and were barely able to clear the trees. If I could have stood on the wing of the plane, I would have been able to pick leaves.

Luther was a highly skilled pilot, or we probably would not be here. I said: "Great job, Luther." He did not answer me. For years afterwards, I thought that it had been somewhat of a routine flight for him.

Many years later my good friend and coworker, Ted, and I were in Michigan for our regional meeting held in Jenison, Michigan where Cal lived. Ted was now a licensed pilot, and on the way back I stopped at Luther's home to introduce him to Ted. When a non pilot introduces two pilots to each other, he better keep his mouth shut.

They talked to each other for well over a half hour and I had said very little. Luther began to tell Ted about our experience by telling him that I was the only one that had flown under utility wires with him and that it had been his first time also! He continued to tell Ted about the experience by saying that he was sweating blood, ready to mess his pants, and that I was calmly sitting beside him, totally unconcerned.

Out of Body Experience

During the summer of 1993, I was scheduled to attend a conference in Boulder. It was for a week, and I made arrangements for my wife and I to stay in a nearby timeshare for the week before the conference. I also chose to drive.

I was trying to lose some weight and was doing so, but, on our way to Colorado I began to drink much water and rush to the rest areas. Marilyn, who is a nurse, told me to have the doctor check me for diabetes when we returned home.

Immediately after returning home I left for another meeting in New York. I asked Don, a fellow sales rep, about a hernia that he had to have repaired. I had a small bulge that was appearing since I had lost weight. He also told me to see a doctor.

When I returned home, I made an appointment to see a surgeon, and after he examined me, he told me that I was to have immediate surgery.

I had seen him on a Monday, and I spent the week working in my storage area lifting books, and getting ready for the school year. I also played some golf and was doing some paperwork on Friday morning, when he called and asked me if I knew that I was a diabetic. I told him that Marilyn had been telling me that I was, but, that I had not been checked for it.

I asked him what my sugar reading was, and he told me that it was 400. I asked him what it should be, and he said 120. I asked if he was still going to do the surgery, and he told me that I had let that go, and it must be done.

I did not eat anything for twenty-four hours before the surgery was scheduled. On Monday, I went to the hospital for the surgery, and during the surgery, a very surreal thing began to take place. My spirit or conscious part was above the operating table, peering down on a convulsing body, with several nurses trying to hold me down, while the doctor was screaming: "Get dextrose in him now!"

I remember praying to the Lord and telling him that I didn't want to die yet. I was given the dextrose, and the experience was like being thrown into a very hot bath, and then thrown into ice water. My heart felt like it was beating outside of my body.

The surgery was completed, and I woke up in the recovery room with the nurse putting a lancet into my finger, to obtain some blood to check my reading. She continued doing it every ten or fifteen minutes until I was taken to my room.

She told me that I would have to stay in the hospital overnight, and I told her that I was not going to do that. I asked her to bring a wheelchair because I was leaving. I never would have been able to sleep with what they were doing, and I felt Marilyn could monitor me at home.

When I recovered, I asked for a surgery report, and my sugar level had gone from 400 to 20 and back up. I was slow in recovering from having convulsed, but am a firm believer of near death experiences.